Deeper Learning Deeper Leading: Inside Avalon School

Deeper Learning Deeper Leading: Inside Avalon School

Edit by
Walter Enloe

Tertium Quid Press
Saint Paul, Minnesota
2016

Tertium Quid Press
St. Paul, Minnesota 55104

Photographs organized by Serene Enloe
and the students of The Avalon School

Printed in the United States of America
ISBN-13: 978-1533556752
ISBN-10: 153355675X

Deeper Learning, Deeper Leading: Avalon School Project 2016-2017

October 2016

An Invitation to The Avalon Community:

Deeper Learning, Deeper Leading is an Avalon Community project celebrating the school's first fifteen years. The project engages members of the community to document the "Avalon Story," and the project results will include a hard copy and e-book text to be used in celebratory and planning forums in 2017.

Several years ago, in reaction to increasing interest locally, nationally and internationally in Avalon School- its project based learning, student governance and leadership, and teacher ownership and leadership- there was a significant increase in inquiries and visitors. We noted that often they had similar interests and questions. So we decided to create a compilation of selected articles written about the school and program to help interested folks prepare for their visits. The "first edition" was prepared as an e-book in 2013 and was titled I*nside Avalon: Creating and Sustaining a Democratic Community* (and is found on the Avalon School website: go to Prospective Students, Awards and Recognition, Inside Avalon).

Inside Avalon, today revised and updated to some degree, forms the basis of this current "galley proof" text, *Deeper Learning, Deeper Leading,* celebrating the first fifteen years of the school. Over the next few months we invite the Avalon Community to join us in a variety of ways to complete this project: writing personal testaments and recollections, editing contributions including determining inclusions, deletions, formatting; deciding on captions for student photographs taken this spring. And developing plans for sharing and utilizing the book in the spring of 2017 both to celebrate Avalon's past and to reflect on its future.

In a word *Deeper Learning, Deeper Leading* is Avalon community "Project-Based Learning." (PBL) is the curricular core of Avalon. With PBL, students literally design their own education as they brainstorm, design, and execute independent, student-initiated projects. With guidance from advisors, PBL allows students to engage deeply in their study while learning independence and self-direction."

Avalon alumni, parents, staff, students and friends.

Funding for this project is provided by the endowed chair in education at HamlineUniversity, the Gordon B. Sanders Chair, in honor of Hamline's original sponsorship of the school beginning in 2001.

Questions/ Suggestions: please contact:
Nora (nora@ avalonschool.org) or
Walter (wenloe@ hamline.edu)

Deeper Learning, Deeper Leading: Avalon School Project

"Project-Based Learning (PBL) is the curricular core of Avalon. With PBL, students literally design their own education as they brainstorm, design, and execute independent, student-initiated projects. With guidance from advisors, PBL allows students to engage deeply in their study while learning independence and self-direction."

Deeper Learning, Deeper Leading is a Avalon Community project celebrating the school's first fifteen years. The project engages members of the community to document the "Avalon narrative," and the project includes a hard-copy and e-book text to be used in critical and celebratory forums in 2017

15th Anniversary Text (hard copy/ e-book) for March 2017

Phase 1 Due for October 6

1. A Working Galley Proof prototype
2. Display for Oct 6 gathering
3. Invitation to Avalon Community to join the project (handout; on-line sign-up)
4. Needed contributions content narratives: testaments from community members, present, alumni students and parents and staff
5. Photo captions
6. Editing
7. Additions/deletions
8. Assistance with Dominic production design

Phase 2 Due for February 15, 2017

1. Completed text for distribution
2. Invitation to join circles (read text, discussion, strategic planning, etc)

Phase 3

1. Forum/events last week of March, 2017

About The Photographs

many of us live in (and some of us try to avoid) a 21st world of instantaneous communication and gratification. Social media with Facebook, Twitter, YouTube, blogs and microblogs, Google, Linkedin, Pineterest, Tumble or Instagram using iPads, Tables, iPhones or Smartphones. Many of us are seeking a respite from Social media whether unplugging ourselves or seeking Tech-Free Camps and Digital Detox retreats and yet, we live in a world of Selfies, intangible and impermanent.

The Avalon book project invited students to replace their iPhones with Polaroid cameras. Retro analog versus digital. Our motto: Take a Picture. It lasts longer. Film documents the immediate environment in real time. With an instant film photograph, you get what you get. You can't alter or "photoshop" it while it develops in your hands, before your eyes. It's a tangible document of a chosen moment. The moment was specifically chosen because it had some kind of meaning for the photographer. So students at Avalon captured pictures of their daily lives at school through the medium of instant format film.

We bought five students, volunteers for the project, Fuji Instax mini cameras and film packs. We invited them to meet as we explored the mission behind the project, background information on instant film photography, how to use the camera, and procedures how to choose the best shots showcasing their everyday experiences at school. Lastly, scanning, cropping and editing techniques were introduced. Students were able to produce a body of work illustrating the unique place we call Avalon. Next steps is to give narrative voice to each of the photos.

- Serene and Walter Enloe

Chapter 1

Deeper Learning Deeper Leading: The Avalon School Community

Walter Enloe, August 30, 2016

We, the people of Avalon, in order to provide for a safe and productive learning environment, promote the obtaining and usage of knowledge for the benefit of those around us, and ensure general happiness, do ordain and establish this constitution for Avalon High School. 2002

-Avalon High School Constitution, 2002

In 1995 I was asked to consult with a couple of entrepreneurs and a fledgling parent group to create new schools through Minnesota's public chartering initiative. I began my career in 1971 at the founding of the progressive, open school The Paideia School in Atlanta teaching every grade level K-12 through 1980 as I completed my Ph.D. studying the constructivist epistemology and human development theory of Jean Piaget and its corresponding activity pedagogy. Those experiences led me to Hiroshima where for eight years I was lead teacher and principal establishing the school as an accredited, nonprofit institution with an ethos and international curriculum predating the International Baccalaureate's primary years program (the ICDP, The International Curriculum Development Project through the European Council of International Schools). I was then invited to be Senior Fellow in Global Education the first years of the University of Minnesota's Center for Applied Research and Educational Improvement (CAREI) and then its director of the rural component (three Minnesota school districts) of the National Models School Project in Global Education (led by Wilard Kneip and John Goodlad). Along with several other grassroots school development projects I joined SchoolStart to create and sustain what became Twin Cities Academy (1999) and then Avalon School (2001). In each of these cases I was motivated by two insights or visions of what education (and thus schooling) should be: first, Article 26 of the Universal Declaration of Human Rights (1948) which reads in part, "*Education shall be directed to the full development of the human personality, and to the strengthening of respect for human rights and fundamental freedoms.*" And Piaget's argument that "*the principal goal of education is to create people who are capable of doing new things, not simply repeating what other generations have done- people who are creators, inventors and discoverers. The second goal of education is to form minds that are critical, can verify, and do not accept everything they are offered. The great danger today is from slogans, collective opinions, ready-made trends of thought. We have to be able to resist individually, to criticize, and to distinguish between what is proven and what is not. So we need pupils who are active, who learn early to find out for themselves, partly by their own spontaneous activity and partly through the materials we set up for them, who learn early to tell what is verifiable and what is simply the first idea to come to them.* (Personal communication, 1977).

Finally from those experiences in Hiroshima at the hypocenter of Ground Zero and in the aftermath of 9-11 (my mother's birthday and the first weeks of the opening of Avalon School) I made a personal commitment to support in every way I could in the decades following the United Nations Nobel Peace Prize laureates' 1998 declaration, "To Create a Culture of Peace and Nonviolence for The Children of The World."

These commitments then, brought me to the wonderful community we call Avalon and has sustained my involvement the past fifteen years as the school community continues to live out daily its mission: *Avalon School prepares students for college and life in a strong, nurturing community that inspires active learning, engaged citizenship, and hope for the future.*

In the spring of 2001 I sent out a postcard to thousands of teachers in Minnesota (thanks to Hamline University's continuing studies office) inviting "passionate, inspired, hard-working" teachers to join us. It read in part: **What if teachers could design the ideal school? We can!** And we have the past fifteen years accomplished what we set out to do: *to build an imaginative, creative, disciplined learning community.*

Global Teacher Global Learner

Years ago I co-taught a course with David Selby and Graham Pike from the Centre for Global Education, University of York; I was then lead teacher and head of Hiroshima International School and an associate of the University of Minnesota's Global Education Center. From these two wonderful teacher-learners I articulated an essential insight into the power of authentic, experiential learning which I had experienced previously in such diverse learning experiences as earning Boy Scout merit badges to studying in college one subject in-depth over a month ("Winter Term"). Let me paraphrase from their seminal text, *Global Teacher, Global Learner* (1988). In most schools today (2016) learning about is the predominant mode. Essentially it is a knowledge-oriented process concerned with the assimilation and interpretation of concepts, data, evidence and facts. In some classrooms students also experience the learning for approach through the acquisition or development of skills (e.g., research and communication skills) enabling them to apply the knowledge they have gained. Rarely, however, do they experience *learning in or learning through*, "whereby the actual process of learning is also a significant part of the intended substance of learning,"(p. 49).

From a global education perspective consider learning experiences on the topic of human rights that clarify these three modes in the classroom. Students will learn about the key international documents on human rights (such as The United Declaration of Human Rights, and the Convention in the Rights of The Child), principal concepts such as civil and political rights, social and economic rights, due process, fair treatment, etc.; perhaps they explore the violation of human rights through various case studies (Mahatma Gandhi, Martin Luther King, Nelson Mandela, Aung San Suu Kyi). *Learning for* human rights will require not only the acquisition of essential knowledge, but the development and practice of the skills necessary to promote and defend human rights. These

skills would include effective communication skills, as well as co-operation, negotiation and decision-making skills, and hopefully, campaigning and non-violent action skills. *Learning in and learning through* human rights goes one stage or level deeper.

Knowledge and skills learning is reinforced through the very taproot of the learning experience: the nature of the learning context where the quality of the learning experience has a direct bearing on the quality of learning. In other words the medium of experience is a message of that experience: how one experiences learning is part of what one learns. That is, the quality of interpersonal relationships and the methods of learning and teaching exhibit an intrinsic respect for the rights (and responsibilities) of learners-as-teachers and teachers-as-learners. In the global classroom then, where mediums and messages harmonize, *learning in or learning through* is the prevailing mode, the deeper learning and leading.

Learning as a Way of Leading

In their groundbreaking book *Learning As A Way of Leading: Lessons From The Struggle for Social Justice* (2009) Stephen Preskill and Stephen Brookfield take an in-depth look at how social justice leaders (from Ella Banks, Septima Clark to Myles Horton) learn, how they support other people's learning, and how this deepens their social impact. As the authors explain the best leaders enjoy a capacity to be taught, to work collaboratively with followers, to listen and learn from people around them, and in many cases, to lead by being led. Such leaders are developmental leaders, chiefly interested in drawing out (educing) the abilities and capacities of their followers. They do this by remaining open to what those followers can impart to them as much as by guiding them to new possibilities. But from a broader perspective this text tells the stories of many community and organizational leaders who share a common commitment to leading through deeper learning. These leaders, some without formal positional authority or portfolio, share common capacities, dispositions and practices upon which their success is dependent. The authors conceive of these commonalities as the nine learning tasks or habits of leadership (which are paraphrased from p.15-18). Foundational to all of the tasks is: 1) *learning how to be open to the contributions of others.* This practice makes the second leadership task possible, 2) *learning how to reflect critically on one's practice.* Inextricably bound together, only if one is open to others' contributions can you develop the perspective required for critical reflection. 3) *Learning how to support the growth of others* deepens leadership and enhances learning such that traditional job appraisals of "how well did you do your job?" are supplanted by " what and how did you learn in your job?" Supporting each other is connected with the fourth leadership task, 4) *learning how to develop collective leadership.* "Collective leadership flows from a culture in which engagement in, and sharing of, learning is an expectation and a priority. As people learn new skills, dispositions, and epistemologies, they inevitably become aware of how individual learning is both premised on and contributes to the learning of others."

Once we understand that so much of the deep taproot of our identity, our strength and our learning is the collective, we realize that leadership resides in the collective itself. "We cannot learn to be critically reflective, analyze experience, question ourselves, practice democracy, sustain hope, or create community without the necessary involvement of others." This collaborative, group leadership task is interconnected to the leadership practices of 5) *learning how to analyze experience* and 6) *learning how to question oneself and others.* The seventh task of learning leadership is 7) *learning democracy,* what the authors refer to as "the central task of adult life." In order to live democratically one must learn among others "to honor diversity, live with the partial functioning of the democratic ideal, avoid the trap of false antithesis...accept the compatibility of ends and means....and appreciate the comedy inherent in democracy's contradictions." When efforts to live democracy fully inevitably fail, the eighth task 8) *learning to sustain hope in the face of struggle.* Finally the ninth leadership practice 9) *learning to create community.* "Building communities in which the members of these communities are authentically empowered to make important decisions for themselves and their (fellow citizens) remains a chief objective of the work of leaders who learn." Deeper learning, deeper leading!

Deeper Learning

In Deeper Learning: How Eight Innovative Public Schools Are Transforming Education in The Twenty-First Century (2014) Monica Martinez and Dennis McGrath provide concrete examples (Avalon School is one of the eight schools profiled) of what deeper, student and community centered learning (often referred to as "high impact learning") looks like, feels like, smells like as living organizations.

All of the schools are based upon these shared principles:

1. Establish cohesive, collaborative learning communities that sharply differ from the top-down national norm

2. Empower and encourage students to be more self-directed, creative, and cooperative by getting them out of their chairs and more directly involved in their own education
3. Make curricula more engaging, memorable, and meaningful, by integrating subjects and establishing relevance to real-world concerns
4. Reach outside classroom walls to extend the idea and purpose of learning beyond school, forming partnerships with businesses, organizations, research institutions, and colleges and universities
5. Inspire students by endeavoring to understand their talents and interests, customizing learning wherever possible to discover the motivational 'hook' for each young person
6. Incorporate technology purposefully to enhance, rather than simply automate, learning.

Martinez argues while much of society has radically changed in the past twenty years with the advent of the Information Age, the great majority of pubic schools hold on to early 20th century practices, programs, and organizations ((similarly documented by Philip Jackson, Life in Classrooms (1968) and John Goodlad, A Place Called School (1988)). "Teachers lecture while standing in front of rows of desks, students take notes with pencils and lug heavy books, and both groups expect students to memorize content more often than to learn or practice new skills. In general, students are trained to act as followers, not leaders." (my italics)

Deeper Learning Deeper Leading

In his seminal essay "The Right to Education in the Modern World," the eminent human scientist Jean Piaget explicates Article 26 of the UN Declaration of Human Rights (1948) which reads in part: *Education shall be directed to the full development of the human personality and to the strengthening of respect for human rights and fundamental freedoms. Education's goal is to create* individuals capable of intellectual and moral autonomy and of respecting this autonomy in others by applying the rule of reciprocity that makes it legitimate for themselves. (in *To Understand Is To Invent: The Future of Education*, 1973). This goal for education raises a fundamental pedagogical problem: **Is it possible to form autonomous personalities by means of techniques that entail intellectual and/or ethical restrictions to differing degrees?** *Or isn't there a contradiction in terms since personality development really requires a free and spontaneous activity in a* *social milieu based upon collaboration and not submissiveness? It becomes evident that neither the teacher's authority nor the best lessons he can give on the subject suffices to engender living, dynamic relationships, comprised of both independence and reciprocity. Only a social life among the students themselves-that is, self-government taken as far as possible and parallel to the intellectual work carried out in common- will lead to the double development of personalities, masters of themselves and based on mutual respect (p.110).*

What is the best method to make a student a future good citizen? *Is it simply to give him, for a certain number of hours a year, a systematic course of 'civic instruction' by describing to him bit by bit the different workings of national institutions that leave him still relatively indifferent, in spite of the eloquence or good will of the teacher? Or is it to graft such training onto the experience of self-government in the school so that the child knows by experience what an executive committee, a general assembly, and a court are, and can be interested in analogous institutions at a level he could never imagine without such analogies? We even maintain that if it should be necessary to sacrifice the teaching of 'civic instruction' to the practice of self-government, the latter would produce better citizens than the finest lessons, and that if these lessons are given without social experience to support them, their practical results risk being of little worth. (p. 130).*

Avalon: Participatory Centered Learning Community

- Public chartering majority teachers on board of directors
- Cooperative model
- Faculty leadership of all stakeholders (e.g. EAs have an equal vote)
- School constitution with four branches government

1. We the people
2. Congress makes laws/rules (students)
3. Executive branch (teachers with veto power of Congress' laws/rules
4. Peer mediation/restorative justice circles to resolve issues between congress and executive branch

David Tyack & Larry Cuban in *Tinkering Toward Utopia: A Century of Public School Reform* (1997) contend that American education has vacillated between student centered and teacher directed emphases, a cyclical pendulum of one socio-political perspective dominating the other; reform efforts demonstrating the most promise, however, has been more participatory centered, with equity between all stakeholders as found in Barbara Rogoff's classic study, *Learning Together: Children and Adults in a School Community* (2002), and as exemplified at Avalon School's 2016 website logo: **Deeper Learning Deeper Leading Own Your School** (a message to all stakeholders: parents, students, teachers).

In an earlier publication, *Learning Circles* (1988) we aimed to capture the many lessons we have learned from working with people, younger and older alike, with the concept of learning circles, defined as small communities of learners who come together purposefully to support each other in the process of learning; these circles vary in membership and duration yet they hold fast to leadership through intentionality, purpose and learning. These circles capture the essence of interdependence found in natural ecological systems (we refer to this phenomenon as taking the organism seriously in organizations), especially those principles of diversity of thought, energy flow, sustainability and co-evolution or leading and learning together. Capra in *The Web of Life* (1996) points out that the purpose of life is learning- and that learning is constructivist for all living systems.

Learning circles, whether Avalon seminars or collaborative projects, or faculty study and work groups, exude leadership as participants have choice, take responsibility for their own development, and set their own agendas. Linda Lambert (p. x) writes, "As they explore and create these three freedoms (choice, responsibility, agenda setting) they perform as a professional culture," a professional culture of leaders that is directly related to student achievement and deep empowerment of themselves as leaders through: 1) shared decision making; 2) a shared sense of purpose; 3) collaborative work toward that purpose; and 4) collective responsibility. To lead it is essential to recognize that learning and leadership are inextricably intertwined. To lead is to engage community participants in the process of making meaning- the process of learning toward purpose. The essence of deeper learning, deeper leading is responsibility for the learning of other shareholders in the culture, and for the learning organization as a whole.

In a recent publication by Teachers College Press, *Restoring Dignity in Public Schools: Human Rights Education in Action* (2016) Maria Hantzopoulos cites a case-study of the Humanities Preparatory Academy in New York City and how it has developed an urban school demonstrating how to create a vibrant, authentic learning community. "Drawing from rich narratives of human rights education (HRE) in action, the author shows how school leaders can create an environment in which a culture of dignity, respect, tolerance, and democracy flourishes." In the chapter T*he Components of Participation: Schooling That Fosters Democracy and Student Agency* she elaborates in great detail how the use of student advisories, town meetings, Quad gatherings (four advisories convene around a certain issue or topic), and the "fairness committee" utilizing restorative approaches all operate in tandem to constitute a living democracy much like Avalon School (however the Avalon learning community is even more enhanced by a working constitution, branches of government involving all stakeholders, as well as a teacher cooperative and staff meetings modeling democratic processes).

Currently 2016 at-play terminology and labeling for the school reform work Avalon is connected with and influential in Teacher Power/ Teacher Led Schools/ EDVisions CES Leader Center/ Innovative Schools Network among others focus on teacher leadership and project based learning. But seldom do I find folks concerned with either the school's development as project-based learning and leadership, and seldom do we find a school ethos held by teachers that students are emerging leaders where the purpose of a "teacher powered" school is not only teacher empowerment and efficacy and well-being- if they "own" it they'll be more accountable and responsible- but to foster deeper learning and leading in the students themselves. An essential insight from our work with learning communities (Learning Circles 1998 and the years following) is that the conditions we identified as keys to authentic, sustained professional development and ownership can be applied to the students and most participants want deeper learning to facilitate deeper leading and thereby characterize the whole learning, leading organization. The six conditions: assessing expectations, supporting learners, documenting public work, building community, constructing knowledge, changing. growing, developing school culture.

Joel Westheimer in *What Kind of Citizen?: Educating Our Children for The Common Good* (2015) with his colleague Joel Kahne have spent years studying a variety of programs focused on developing good citizenship skills and concepts among young adults and youth. "In study after study, we came to similar conclusions: the kinds of goals and practices commonly represented in school programs that hope to foster democratic citizenship have more to do with voluntarism, charity, and obedience than with democracy. In other words, 'good citizenship' to many educators means listening to authority figures, being nice to neighbors, and helping out at a soup kitchen- not grappling with the kinds of social only decisions that every citizen in a democratic society needs to learn how to do."(p. 37). In their studies they found that three different but connected visions of citizenship were helpful in making sense of the programs they studied as they posed this question: *What kind of citizen do we need to support an effective democratic society?* They identified three visions of "good citizens" from these largely high school programs: *the Personally Responsible Citizen, the Participatory Citizen, and the Social Justice-Oriented Citizen.* An" ideal" "portrait" of the public 'make the world a better place' citizen would be the integration of these three kinds of citizens, each defined by core assumptions of action roles in the community. 1. The personally responsible citizen acts responsibly in the community to solve social problems and improve society; the citizen must have good character-try must be honest, responsible, law-abiding members of the community. 2. The participatory citizen is an active member of community organizations and/or improvement efforts. To solve social problems and improve society, citizens must actively participate and take leadership positions within established systems and community structures. 3. The social justice-oriented citizen critically assesses social, political, and economic functions and structures. To solve public social problems and improve society, citizens must question and change established systems and structures when they reproduce patterns of injustice over time (p.39).

All of these kinds of citizenship are found within the Avalon community, both in its ethos and its curriculum, What is unique, I think, is that adults constitute a learning community of participatory citizenship and leadership that has personal citizenship dimensions and social justice orientations and commitments. The functional organizational components operate as an interactive, dynamic whole: the chartering governance of teachers, parents and community folk; the teachers' cooperative and decision-making practices; the students' choices for study, participation and leadership;

and the collective union of governance through the school constitution of "We the people of Avalon" with its executive, legislative, and judicial functions and structures. In Harry Boyte's terms the school is "living democracy daily" with both teachers and students separately and collectively, "making the rules."

Avalon School engages students in deeper learning, which begins with deeper leading, and reciprocally deeper leading grows through deeper learning, knowing, and understanding. Students and teachers alike are empowered to lead their education work and to accept personal & shared responsibility for their community of learners and citizens. As leaders and shared decision-makers they become personally accountable and responsible for the self, for others, and for the whole. A key insight from Avalon is that leading and learning are inextricably and continually bound in an organic web of mutuality and reciprocity in which leadership can be taught for the common good in a complex, changing world. (see Sharon Parks' Leadership Can Be Taught (2005) on the work of Ron Heifetz).

Finally Rebecca Raby (2012) in *School Rules: Obedience, Discipline and Elusive Democracy's* chapter "Students Having a Say" quotes Hughes and Carrico's case study of the participatory rights and responsibilities cultivated through deeper learning and leading at Windsor House School in Vancouver, B.C. *"It is ironic that in a society that sees itself as democratic, it would be taken for granted that children should be raised under conditions of virtual dictatorship. Giving children an equal right to participate in setting the standards and guidelines by which they live seems necessary if they are to mature into adults that are capable of participating in a genuine democracy. Windsor House (a democratic in North Vancouver) is hardly without rules; there are plenty. The important thing is that anyone who dislikes a rule is free to gather support to change it."*

The school's liberationist worldview is consonant with the *United Nations Convention on the Rights of The Child.* Articles 12, 13 and 14 ensure children's rights to freedom of expression, to rights to be heard, and rights for children to participate in decision-making that affects their immediate lives; and includes a developmental provision that as young people age they should have increasing rights and responsibilities of involvement in decisions that affect them (even though in most schools the opposite is actualized; that is, the older children become there seem to be fewer opportunities to participate authentically in governance and self-determination).

How Avalon School Defines Deeper Learning, Deeper Leading (from www.projectfoundry.com)

Deeper Learning For Students

Many educators acknowledge students should graduate with 21st century skills like perseverance, self-direction, planning, self-discipline, adaptability, and initiative. However, in many schools, students are not empowered to practice these skills. Everyday our job at Avalon is to empower students and personalize learning. Students learn skills to mediate conflict. solve problems, and create new rules through our Avalon Congress. With teacher support, students determine their own curriculum and decide how they will meet graduation standards through seminars or independent projects. Deeper learning requires that teachers know their students and connect them to relevant learning opportunities.

Deeper Leading For Teachers

While students are empowered to lead their education and accept responsibility for the community of learners in the school, teachers at Avalon are similarly empowered. There is no principal or director, but the staff operates as leaders and shared decision-makers. At Avalon, teachers accept greater accountability for school success and control the curriculum. budget, professional development, and personnel decisions. It is in our hands to meet academic and school goals. Our model of Deeper Leading contributes to powerful teacher retention.

Chapter 2

New Tools for Teacher-Powered Schools

Carrie Bakken

Imagine you're a 6th grader in suburban Minnesota. You have a seat near the classroom window. One afternoon, you see a motorcycle pull up to your school, rev the engine, and wave in your direction. Your teacher grabs her things and exits. Your classmates rush to the window, just in time to watch your teacher jump on the back of the motorcycle. Gretchen Sage-Martinson always remembered her 6th grade teacher's dramatic exit from the teaching profession. Twenty years later in 2001, Sage-Martinson—by then a teacher herself—helped hire the first faculty for Avalon School in St. Paul, Minn., including me.

The Retention Problem and Reform Solution

Teachers do not always leave the profession with early-1980s rebel flair, but we do leave—and in staggering numbers. In a March 2015 interview on NPR, researcher Richard Ingersoll noted that teacher turnover costs exceed 2 billion dollars per year. Ingersoll also asserted, "One of the reasons teachers quit is that they feel they have no say in decisions that ultimately affect their teaching."

Some education reform policies make matters worse. Strict curriculum guides, excessive testing, and student behavior protocols block teachers from exercising professional autonomy and collaborating in ways that could most benefit students. No wonder so many leave.

But what if teachers could take the reins of reform at the school building level? It's happening right now at Avalon and other teacher-powered schools that offer teachers the collective authority to make decisions influencing their schools' success. More than 75 schools across the country (in rural, urban, and suburban systems and in both unionized district schools and public charters) have adopted the model. And new tools are helping even more educators design (or redesign) their own schools as places that are squarely focused on the needs of students.

Teacher-Powered Accountability

Avalon School serves more than 200 students in grades 6–12 who live in St. Paul, Minneapolis, and the surrounding suburbs. Our student retention rate is more than 90 percent, and our annual teacher retention rate is more than 95 percent. The teacher-powered "model" takes many different forms, with some schools having a principal but allocating certain school decisions to teachers. At Avalon, teachers control all aspects of running our school. Three teachers take on duties as program coordinators, which includes administrative work such as enrollment, testing coordination, and state reporting. Teachers lead as members of the Avalon school board, the finance committee, and the personnel committee. We serve as peer coaches, create marketing materials, write grants, and develop community partnerships. We do all of this—learning new professional skills along the way—while remaining connected to students.

In teacher-powered schools, regardless of the specific governing structure, each staff member must accept ownership, collaborate, solve problems, and hold one another accountable. Teachers control the curriculum, budget, professional development, and personnel decisions, and this means that full responsibility for meeting our academic and school goals is in our hands. All of us must accept ownership for the outcomes—but it is authentic ownership because we help write the goals, determine the academic plan required to achieve them, and adjust accordingly.

Like other public schools in our state, Avalon must meet intense external accountability measures, including 133 graduation standards and hundreds of benchmarks. Students take multiple standardized tests annually. But our most powerful accountability measures are those that we created with students, families, and staff beginning in 2001, including a 300-hour senior project presented to the community. The staff develop relationships with families that result in a 95 percent parent conference participation rate.

Every year, teachers are evaluated on our performance by our colleagues, our students (advisees), and their parents. This level of evaluation and accountability happens in a collaborative environment based on mutual respect for each other's work and was in place long before No Child Left Behind and state-mandated teacher evaluation systems.

The combination of autonomy, collaboration, and accountability is the secret to our retention rate. And a strong retention rate feeds itself, allowing us to implement a strategic plan and continuously improve our learning program, because we know the staff will be there to do the work. It's also cost effective because we are not constantly hiring and mentoring new staff. Avalon School has earned several finance awards from the Minnesota Department of Education and from our charter authorizer because so much of our money goes directly to the classroom.

Empowering Students by Personalizing Learning

Of course, the true appeal of Avalon for me is not the governance structure but what that structure does for students: it allows us, as their teachers, to make decisions that will personalize their learning and also give them the chance to lead.

The first six-week seminar I taught at Avalon was a government class, Freedom and Responsibility. Many of these young adolescents joined my next seminar, Writing the Avalon Constitution, in which they developed a powerful framework for student governance at Avalon while learning about the U.S. government. They defined ownership and accountability and outlined Avalon's three branches of government. They were a source of inspiration as we faced the challenges of putting our new teacher-powered model into action: we realized that if 14- and 15-year-olds could understand the powerful relationship between autonomy and accountability, then adults could, too.

We are a teacher-powered school, but I'd also describe us as student-powered. Students are trusted to learn valuable life lessons, including the idea that with power comes responsibility. They practice mediating conflict, solving problems, and creating new rules through our Avalon Congress. With support from their teachers, students also determine their curriculum and decide how they will meet their graduation standards, whether through seminars or independent projects.

Resources for Going Teacher-Powered

Through the new Teacher-Powered Schools Initiative, pioneers of the model are finding new ways to pass along what we've learned. This partnership between Education Evolving and the Center for Teaching Quality (CTQ) is connecting teachers across the country with potential mentors who have already been there, done that. A growing number of superintendents, principals, union officials, and policymakers are tapping into these resources, too.

Steps to Creating a Teacher-Powered School is an online do-it-yourself guide to starting a school (or reconfiguring an existing one). Crowdsourced from teacher-powered pioneers like my Avalon colleagues and me, the guide covers the big steps—and major decisions—involved in getting your school off the ground. Hundreds of hyperlinked resources let you identify questions to discuss with your cofounders, explore relevant research, and peek at sample governance documents.

An Inventory of Teacher-Powered Schools offers rich information about more than 75 schools like Avalon where the model is already at work. You can ask questions, share resources, and find mentors in a virtual community housed in the CTQ Collaboratory. And a monthly e-newsletter shares information about Twitter chats, conferences, and other events where you can learn more.

Teachers and the Public Are Ready for a New Approach

A recent survey conducted by Education Evolving found that more than half of American teachers are interested in working in a teacher-powered school. Meanwhile, the same survey revealed that 9 in 10 Americans agree that teachers should have more authority in school decision making.

Public demand for teacher-powered schools is growing, and as the model spreads, more students and communities will experience the benefits that accrue when schools retain accomplished teachers.

Not all schools must adopt a teacher-powered model, but I would encourage every district to explore the model in at least one school. The sound of students engaged in deeper learning—debating, demonstrating, questioning—as their teachers engage in deeper leading is far more preferable to the squeal of a motorcycle's tires as yet another practitioner flees the profession.*

* Permission to reprint given by ASCD, 2016

Chapter 3

The Origins of Avalon

Carrie Bakken, Nora Whalen, & Gretchen Sage-Martinson - three teachers who played a major role in the creation of Avalon share the story of how the dream became a reality.

The Avalon Charter School opened its doors on Tuesday, September 4, 2001 to 120 ninth and tenth graders from St. Paul, Minneapolis, and the suburban communities surrounding the Twin Cities. To recover the memories of how we opened, especially our first week of school, is to return to experiences of tension, joy, craziness, silliness, mistakes, and successes.

Opening with approximately one year of preparation, from writing initial grants and charter applications to finding a building and hiring staff, Avalon became the seventy-fifth charter school to open in Minnesota, which is the first state to approve charter schools in the nation.

The climate during our start-up efforts was short on legislation and oversight, welcomed innovation, and placed only the slightest emphasis on high-stakes testing. In short, it was an ideal climate for a small group of teachers, parents, community members, and students to dream up their ideal school. Fulfilling this dream, however, required us to separate from the original founders, establish a functioning teacher cooperative, recruit and retain a diverse student body, implement a meaningful project based learning model, and establish a vehicle for student voice. These were clearly daunting tasks, but exciting ones as well. Here was a chance to start a school from scratch; something we had previously only theorized abstractly.

Before prospective families, teachers, and students joined the creation of Avalon, there was a small group of founding members who worked to open the school for a variety of reasons. Unfortunately, many of these reasons were inharmonious. Four founding parents wanted a school where they had a say in who was working with their children, what their children were being taught, and even the daily logistics of the school, such as when the school day started. Other members were expert grant writers who realized that there was money to be made in opening charter schools; they were eager to take advantage of funds being offered by federal and state governments, as well as foundations like The Bill & Melinda Gates and Walton Family foundations. Further, a few others saw Avalon as a possible place for employment, both as educators and managers of the school. With many individuals focused on several different priorities, consensus was difficult. The founders knew that they wanted something different and they were motivated by the sense of innovation that was buzzing around this new model of public education, but they didn't know exactly what innovation would look like. Both collaboration and conflict were rife, as they probably are in any type of creation story. The gap between what the original founders wanted and how they were actually going to actualize it caused a lot of tension, but it was from this tension and pressure that we were eventually able to create Avalon.

Splitting with the Original Founders & the Power of the Teacher Cooperative Model

Early in the start-up process, the grant writers among the founding families applied for a Gates Foundation grant through EdVisions Schools, a Minnesota non-profit educational development organization. Winning the grant a lowed Avalon to develop publicity for the school by using the Gates Foundation name and reputation, but the grant's stipulations also contained leadership and curriculum expectations. The goal of the grant was to essentially replicate Minnesota New Country School located in Henderson, Minnesota. Minnesota New Country School is a rural charter school and one of the first charter schools in the nation. The school gained recognition for project-based learning with a teacher cooperative model; therefore, a school winning this particular Gates grant was required to create both a teacher cooperative model of leadership and a project-based curriculum. In essence, by accepting the Gates grant Avalon answered many of the questions still being debated by its original founders; specifically, questions of leadership organization, and curriculum.

Our early birth as a teacher cooperative almost immediately created tension between the original founders and the three of us, the founding teachers hired to do the work of opening the school. The original founders applied for and accepted the Gates grant, which stipulated a teacher cooperative, but they were neither entirely convinced that the teachers could run the school, nor sure they wanted teachers to run the school.

The founders who were grant writers were thrilled with winning the grant. They believed a teacher cooperative was great. Significantly, though, the grant's requirement was in serious conflict with the business interests of several of the original founders who were interested in the new charter movement for two reasons, the latter of which caused the greatest amount of tension between the founders and founding teachers: an opportunity to start an ideal school for their children and a business opportunity to create a company that would help open new schools.

Like the original founders of Avalon and the students who attend the school, we founding teachers each came to Avalon for different reasons. Nora was in the middle of her third year of teaching when she heard news of Avalon's opening from a flier sent by Hamline University. Having been "pink slipped" her previous two years, Nora was disillusioned by her school's leaders. At the time, the large district for which she worked would again need to make budget cuts and Nora knew that, yet again, her job would probably be in jeopardy.

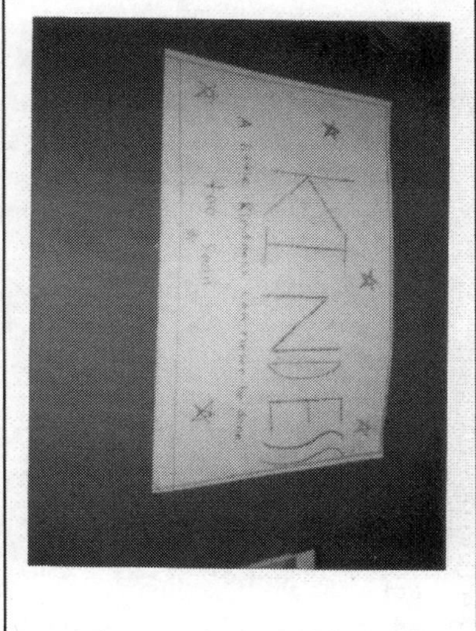

Carrie taught in a small, non-profit alternative school in Minneapolis, which primarily served poor African American students. Although she loved many aspects of her job, especially the students, small class sizes, and classroom autonomy, she could not continue to work at this school because her salary was considerably less than that of even new teachers across the state. With her student loans from a master's in teaching and law school soon due, Carrie sought new employment and haphazardly found Avalon when she responded to an employment ad. She quickly fell in love with the curriculum, the teacher cooperative, and the other teachers hired.

Gretchen found out about Avalon early in the school's starting up process. She had heard from her husband that a group of "idealists" were attempting to create a school that would help to nurture active citizens. Gretchen had worked as a teacher in the Peace Corps as well as in one of Minnesota's largest school districts. She was disheartened with the lack of professional opportunities in the traditional school system. Gretchen had just completed a master's in experiential education when she heard about Avalon, and she was eager to find a place to put some of the interesting, exciting, new theories she had learned into practice.

One of the recruiting methods that Avalon's original founders used during the winter of 2001 was a flier sent out by Hamline School of Education's Professor Walter Enloe, which contained the header "What is Your Ideal School?" This flier drew a talented application pool of experienced teachers seeking a new, innovative, autonomous environment. Teachers were hired with the understanding that they would have significant say in the creation of the school. Visiting Minnesota New Country School in session, spending time at Minnesota New Country School's summer institute, and envisioning a teaching world without assistant principals breathing down our backs was all we needed in order to go full steam ahead. We saw the teacher cooperative as a way to bring a whole new level of challenge, empowerment, and satisfaction to the profession of teaching.

In 2001, Minnesota school charter law required school boards to have a teacher majority as well as parents and community members. As a consequence, in addition to being hired for a start-up charter, we found ourselves sitting on Avalon School's board, a place for even more voice and power. Unfortunately, the tension between the founding teachers who were hired as owners and operators of the school and the business interests of the original founders intensified. We felt strongly that there was no room in the Avalon model for administrative leadership by the original founders, especially because they were not educators.

With each new teacher hire, the original founders lost voice in the governing of the school. As the opening of Avalon drew near, we remained committed to the grant's stipulations and took on more and more of the everyday management of the program, leaving the original founders no choice but to fall back. Eventually, the conflict reached a level where lawyers were brought in and decisions were made using mediation. Those founders who were strongly against the teacher management model eventually left Avalon, taking their children with them.

The teacher cooperative stipulation of the Gates grant was inspiring. But on the ground we realized that to supplement the cooperative, some sort of management system a lowing teachers to do the important job of teaching was necessary. The "co-op" model required that teachers manage the school collaboratively. It meant that Avalon teachers would be in charge of selecting and evaluating fellow staff and determining all aspects of the budget like salaries, transportation, and curriculum expenditures. In accordance with this, as we prepared to open we divided duties and established committees to manage all aspects of the school. Because we were all managers of Avalon, we met daily over the summer and continued to meet daily after school to make decisions.

During the first year, after experiencing some burnout from meeting every day, wellearned to formalize our decision-making process and efficiently facilitate meetings. Today, we only meet once a week as an entire staff to make decisions, and once a week as teachers to improve our practice and participate in professional development as a part of our Learning Program. Although we have made changes to improve our efficiency, after ten years, we continue to run the school as a collaborative.

The Challenge of Recruiting for Avalon

At the time we were trying to open Avalon, unlike students' home districts, Avalon was unproven and therefore risky. Charters were new, teacher co-ops were virtually unheard of, and project based learning just didn't "look" like school to many families.

As we struggled to define what this new school would look like, we began recruiting students. The problem was that the basic logistics of starting up a school had not yet been solved, and this made it difficult to se l Avalon to prospective families. We were still in the process of developing, arguing, and discovering answers for questions from prospective parents like: Where will the school be located? How many staff will be hired? What is the focus of the curriculum? What kind of sports and extra- curricula will be offered? Will busing be available? These questions pertained to significant decisions that needed to be made before enrolling students. It is interesting to note that these unanswered questions did not stop us from holding open houses, trying to se l a somewhat still fictional ideal school, and answering inquiries from prospective parents on the fly with assertions about how we hoped things would go.

By early spring of 2001, we were finally able to sign a lease for a space. Even if we were still working on the how of Avalon, signing a lease at least answered the question of where Avalon would happen,. The school opened in an old coffee warehouse in the Midway neighborhood of St. Paul, the former home of a charter middle school that had failed. Our floor in the building was sandwiched between two established charter schools: an elementary school on the first floor and an alternative high school on the third. To add to the challenge of recruitment, we were located within a district with a great reputation for education, and which appeared to serve most of its population well.

During the time that Avalon was recruiting, it was still relatively early in the "school choice" movement. Most families were relatively satisfied moving through their home districts and sending their children to the schools to which they had been assigned based on attendance boundaries. For families to begin to think about Avalon as a school option, families had to first realize the problems with traditional educational models, next they had to want something different, and finally they had to have the resources of time and access in order to become aware of the fact that school choice existed, particularly choices beyond expensive, private schools. Ultimately, Avalon attracted the racially and economically diverse student body for which we had hoped, but in the early days the school's model appealed mostly to white, middle class families who had the time and resources to access innovative educational opportunities like Avalon.

Fortunately for Avalon, a small group of families from a creative middle school in a nearby suburb of St. Paul chose Avalon for their ninth graders. These families were familiar with the process of exercising their right to choose a school for their children because they had already chosen to attend their previous school, Crosswinds Middle School in Woodbury,

Minnesota. Crosswinds is an inter-district public school that families can choose to attend. The families that first came to Avalon from Crosswinds were thrilled with Avalon's highly individualized project based learning model. These families became very active in recruiting, hiring, and building the Avalon community and their children served as student representatives on our earliest hiring committees. In fact, these students also stuffed envelops for mailings, recruited students, built furniture, and set up computers so that Avalon could open in September.

Because we felt the need to get the word out about our school (even though we were still conflicted about what that word should really be) we approved an early student-recruiting flier that boldly stated, "A Public School with a Private School Feel." At this point in time, the only real alternatives to the traditional schools in Minnesota were exclusive private schools or public Alternative Learning Centers. This latter group of schools served the students who could or would not make it in traditional school programs. Alternative Learning Centers had the reputation of being holding zones, where students disillusioned and bored with the traditional educational models passed the time before they either matriculated out of the system by age, or earned a G.E.D. We didn't necessarily want to be thought of as a lofty private school, and although we didn't want Avalon to be understood as a traditional alternative school, we did want it to be understood as an alternative to traditional educational models.

Considering the lack of any other details, "A Public School with a Private School Feel" spoke more powerfully than we intended. Avalon was trying to recruit as many students as possible. Although we were not trying to recruit specific types of students, this flier spoke loudly to those families to whom Avalon was either intentionally or unintentionally catering. These first public words about Avalon—"A Public School with a Private School Feel"— alluded to elitist, expensive programs even though our intention was more to differentiate us from alternative and traditional educational models.

Today, we marvel at the early open houses. How did we convince parents to send their kids to Avalon without a proven track record? We advertised in newspapers and hung posters, but both Avalon and charter schools were far from household words. Once families found out about us they had to be willing to sign up their child, pull them out of their school, and take a risk on something that had no sense of security. Avalon had no graduating classes and there were no guarantees of college acceptance. In the beginning, the families who found us were those who had connections in the educational world and the resource of spare time to find educational options for their children.

Our recruitment efforts relied heavily on our own enthusiasm for project based learning and the previous success of Minnesota New Country School. The project-based learning program spoke to families who knew Montessori, Waldorf, the Un- Schooling Movement, and active homeschoolers. Many families came to us because traditional school was not working for their kids. Many students coming to us had been disengaged learners in their former schools who suffered from depression and anxiety in response. Families of these students were desperate to find new options for their kids. We couldn't promise Spanish or French, calculus, or any sort of sports program, but we could promise individualized learning and attention to each family's needs. Families heard this loud and clear, and they responded.

As teachers, we felt we were offering a new type of school that would really work for students disaffected by traditional educational programs. We envisioned being a welcoming place for a diverse group of learners who were beaten down by trying to fit into a system that didn't cater to their needs. An early article about Avalon in The Edge newspaper, a publication distributed in organic food co-ops and other new-age businesses, helped us secure a number of families with students who learned differently and who were open to new models of education. We also recruited at District 202, an after-school community center for queer youth. At District 202 we attracted several students looking for a school community that was more accepting of who they were.

We also made efforts to recruit from more racially diverse communities by taking out ads in Spanish language newspapers and hiring a Hmong recruiter to work on recruiting from St. Paul's large Hmong community St. Paul is home to the second largest Hmong refugee community in the U.S. In 2001, the year in which Avalon opened, the U.S. Census estimated that the Hmong population in St. Paul increased almost 150 percent since 1990. Our recruiter attracted and enrolled 15-20 Hmong families, about fifteen percent of the first year's student body. But by November of the first year, many of these students drifted back to their neighborhood schools. The recruiter explained to us that, in the end, many Hmong families were not willing to take a risk on a school that did not have a demonstrated history of success.

Before opening, our recruiter strongly encouraged us to contract with the St. Paul Public Schools bus service so that students could be bused to Avalon. Working around the SPPS' schedule would have forced us to start our school day before 7:00 AM or after 10:00 AM. Instead, we opted to spend our transportation budget on the Twin Cities public transit system, which a lowed us greater flexibility, but this was one more break away from the traditional look of schooling. We saw using Metro Transit busing as a good decision, because it gave teachers control of the school day. We didn't imagine the implications of our decisions. According to our recruiter, many Hmong families understood the fact that we did not use the district's transportation system as a lack of security, safety, and reliability.

Another hurdle we encountered in the recruitment process was educating all prospective families about the benefits of project based learning while we as teachers were also learning about the methodology. Our visits to Minnesota New Country School inspired us and we were excited about the opportunities and advantages of the model. The broader project based learning model that Avalon eventually adopted melded well with Minnesota's Profiles of Learning—state legislation that required two basic tests and twenty-three performance-based standards for all public schools. The summer before we opened the teachers did minimal, specific curricular preparation because we planned to develop an individualized curriculum with each student. During the summer, teachers brainstormed how the school would establish protocols and practices that would elicit students' voices and help them develop a sense of responsibility to their own education.

Circle Dances and Rituals of Creativity vs. the Realities of Empowering Students

Is it too much to ask students in ninth and tenth grade to create a document for decision-making? Is it too much to ask them to create a school? Set cultural norms? Create their own curriculum and take control of their learning? The answer to these questions is definitely No. And that summer before opening we worked hard to build the kind of scaffolding students could use to design and implement their own individualized education. As we planned, we imagined that students would come to us with a good deal of project management prowess. We envisioned a l-school meetings where students shared their innermost desires and passionately discussed how and what they were learning. We went so far as to imagine bizarre circle dances and rituals of creativity and expression. And we assumed we would all work together peacefully in a wonderful new learning community.

Very quickly it was September of 2001 and those most important members of our community, the students, walked through the doors. Although we thought we could throw one hundred students onto the floor of a building and ask them to talk about creating their own learning community; needless to say, the students' responses in that first circle convinced us that we were far from ever having ritual circle dances. We saw that our new community of twenty-first-century learners was made up of one hundred very individual students. These students found themselves at Avalon for one hundred different reasons and with just as many attitudes. Thankfully, some of these students came to Avalon specifically to answer the same question posed by staff members: What is your ideal school? While the students' questions were not as touchy-feely as the staff's, our two views were not so far apart.

The question for Avalon staff has never been whether students may have a voice in the school, but how much of a voice and what the process is for exercising it? The students struggled with the same questions, and in those first few days a small group of them started to campaign for a traditional student council with a student government and elections for class president. This campaign produced several mainstays of the present Avalon community including the school's constitution. As we created a school that provides students voice in their own education, the adults and students in the Avalon community were required to challenge their own traditional views of adolescence, democracy, and adult-child power relations that exist in traditional education models. The creation of the Avalon Constitution very much documents these challenges.

During the first six weeks of school, the Advisory Council and Student Government emerged out of our community discussions regarding power, student voice, and process. The Advisory Council was a group of self-selected students from each advisory; they met with Avalon's lead teacher, Andrea Martin, and Carrie, a social studies advisor. The students discussed problems and issues within the school and they proposed solutions. The student government group spent most of its energy event planning and creating a student election. After a few weeks of wondering how these groups would work together, the school community (teachers and students alike) decided we needed a document outlining student input and decision-making. Dr. Walter Enloe, a Hamline University professor and advisor to Avalon, suggested wellook at other schools' constitutions, such as the one from Paideia School in Atlanta, Georgia. The constitutions of schools like Paideia were helpful to us in creating a unique document reflective of both Avalon's distinctive educational environment, the student community that designed the school's Constitution, and the exacting though stimulating process students used to create it.

Avalon's Constitution was born out of a six-week seminar on the U.S. government. About twenty-five students volunteered to participate in the seminar aptly titled, "U.S. Government: Writing the Avalon Constitution." In the seminar, the students dissected the U.S. Constitution while Carrie facilitated discussions. Importantly, Carrie did not write a word of the final Avalon Constitution. Instead, every day a ninth grader took notes on the students' ideas and wrote the final document. Emerging out of a school climate where student empowerment was an expectation, the final Avalon Constitution included a formal process for creating school norms and decision-making, and the same students who participated in the U.S. Government seminar also wrote Avalon's governance model.

When given the opportunity, Avalon students created a thoughtful decision-making Constitution. This document helped students to design a strong Gay Straight Alliance and Peer Sexual Health Educators group as well as encourage a positive, inclusive school culture for all students, particularly those with disabilities and those who had been bullied or marginalized in their former schools.

Staying True to Avalon Despite the Pressures of State Mandates

There are underlying questions regarding student empowerment at Avalon that we continue to discuss during staff meetings. How much control should students have over their education? How much decision-making power should they have? How do we provide a safe learning environment while empowering students to make decisions? How much freedom or supervision do they require? We still wrestle with these questions even as we enter our tenth year.

Although the strong tradition of student empowerment remains at Avalon, in hindsight during our early years students may have been more empowered than they are now. This is because in the beginning of Avalon we relied heavily on the students to actually create the school. Since 2001 when the school opened, new definitions of test-based accountability for teachers and schools have emerged, state mandated curriculum has changed, and the reality of litigation against schools has made empowering adolescents more challenging. Today our students must meet more rigorous and numerous testing benchmarks than they did in 2001. In addition, students must meet new comprehensive graduation requirements, and we know that if we don't meet certain state mandates we could face possible school closure. Unfortunately, because of these state pressures, we don't provide students with the same amount of freedom to fail and or the same amount of space to try new things as we did in the beginning.

Another reason why the freedom to fail and try new things looks different for today's Avalon students is that as a staff and as a school community we are now committed to efficiency—a commitment developed in the early days when we were working to make the teacher cooperative work as an effective model of collaboration and administrative efficiency—and sometimes this commitment entails, perhaps, a bit less student empowerment. When the school first started those early discussions and processes were time intensive. Now when specific issues or ideas emerge regarding student empowerment, almost instinctively those of us who have worked at Avalon since its inception share stories about when the students tried this and failed at that.

Yet as a community, Avalon still values, is committed to, and encourages students to empower themselves. While we want to save students time and possible failure, we work hard to step back in order to a low for community process. This effort continues to be a constant act of self-assessment and improvement for the whole school.

Student Responsibility for the Act of Learning at Avalon

The Avalon School continues to be unique in that it challenges a popular U.S. view of adolescence. Many traditional educational models support a view that requires little of adolescents in order for them to be independent learners. Young people are not trusted with responsibility or decision-making. They are not a lowed to self-regulate. As a culture, we don't hold students accountable for failure. If students fail to perform in school, it is not seen as their failure, but as the failure of the school or teacher. There is another popular idea that some traditional educational programs now use as an argument for the regulation of students. Based on recent brain research demonstrating that the frontal lobes of young people are not fully developed until age twenty or twenty-one, some schools have begun to heavily control and monitor teenagers. One can witness traditional educational programs that are compelled to embrace this view as public schools continue to be required to fo low prescribed state curricula in tightly controlled classrooms and campuses.

Traditional educational models assume that students need to be told what to learn, how to learn, where to learn, and when to learn, but rarely why they are learning. We opened Avalon with the belief that self-regulation, responsibility to others, and accountability are best learned through personal, social, and academic experience. In many traditional public school settings, these experiences are hard to find and undervalued. Giving students the space to meaningfully create a school (an ongoing process), create their education, and make mistakes has a lowed Avalon students to assume responsibility for themselves and their community.

Even as ninth and tenth graders, Avalon students were quite capable of creating their own rigorous education and a school culture that supports it. The rigor came, and still comes, from the conversations we require of each student as he or she proposes and finishes each project. To begin a project and establish its goals and timeline, a student must meet with two advisors who are licensed teachers. The student also establishes the guidelines for how the project will be evaluated at the end of the process. In many ways, the completion of a project is like defending a dissertation in graduate school. The process entails that a student engage in dialogue with the chosen project advisors. Based on product, time logs, and written reflection, the student defends her or his work. The process is labor intensive, reflection intensive, and most importantly, it is community intensive. A student is known at Avalon for the work she or he produces. This concept was new to our ninth and tenth graders in 2001 yet because they had a desire to engage in the process of education, they embraced this philosophy as one that supports learning and individuality.

Through the years, we have reinforced and strengthened our academic requirements. One way in which we have done this is by developing a rigorous senior project requirement that demands that our students design, implement, and showcase a major project in their final year at Avalon. In order to complete this project, each senior gathers a round table of supporters. This round table consists of teachers, parents, and community experts. The adults at the table do not take the lead, but instead respond to the requests, questions, and leadership of the student at the center. These senior projects could not be successful without the larger Avalon community, which is made up of parents, teachers, volunteers, and a variety of community experts. As the student experiences the act of building and strengthening a working, thriving educational community, they identify their own skills and talents as well as gain confidence and experience in being a contributing member of a society. Confidently, Avalon students take these skills with them after graduation.

Ten Years Later

It is now 2010 and the Avalon School has a proven track record of success. Over the past ten years the school has fine-tuned and strengthened its teacher cooperative system, and although our staff has tripled in size, we still make all decisions collaboratively and we all still serve as leaders of the school. As a staff, we have also remained dedicated to empowering students to take charge of their own education despite having to refine the community process we use to inspire and act on this dedication.

With the No Child Left Behind education policy and an ever-increasing emphasis on testing in schools, the temptation to return to the traditional classroom system—where students are the receivers and teachers are the providers of knowledge—is omnipresent and sometimes tempting. But we now have ten years of evidence that highlights the benefits of continuing to empower and challenge adolescents in the ways that we do at Avalon.

It turns out that in the end, what we have created at Avalon is a process through which we guide adolescents to a socially and intellectually responsible adulthood. Instead of our school being a factory-like institution where students move through a system with perhaps a good deal of effort, but no real control, and no real opportunity for empowerment or individuality, Avalon challenges each and every student to figure out who she or he is, and better yet, who she or he wants to become. And importantly, we ask our students how they are going to get there. As in any sound rite of passage for youth, Avalon students are not then left to take on this struggle by themselves, but instead an entire adult community of teachers and parents guide them. After ten years of helping our students negotiate this process, we have found that, maybe surprisingly, it works. As one 2010 graduate describes her experience, Avalon graduates are prepared for their futures, and they are keenly aware of what they want their futures to look like:

I came to Avalon half way through my junior year looking for a challenge. I needed to be more engaged in my education. The Minneapolis Public Schools system had left me with a passive attitude towards high school. My goals were superficial: all I wanted to get out of high school was a good GPA . . . My goals [at Avalon] became significant because my advisors challenged me to do schoolwork that applied to my life outside of school and to the community around me. I learned that grades aren't the most important thing in the world. I was welcomed into a school with a strong, active community and a cooperative, democratic structure. I had a say in how the school ran, and my goals started to extend into Avalon's future. High school became a holistic experience for me because I was encouraged to incorporate what I learned "out there" into my time at Avalon, and to seek out and utilize experts in the community. Watching the senior presentations at the end of the year confirmed the fact that my classmates were incredibly committed to and passionate about their education as well.

After ten years of working together, refining our teacher cooperative and project-based learning model, and committing ourselves to student voice and choice, the students and staff of Avalon have created a community of learners with a democratic model that meaningfully empowers students to take responsibility for their education, for each other, and for the greater community. Like the students who walked through the school's doors in 2001 and shared in its creation, our current students continue to learn that there is meaning and enjoyment in coming together in order to benefit the greater community. They also continue to understand that learning goes far beyond the school classroom and building.

Chapter 4

Changing Relationships in a Project-Based School

Kevin Ward, an Avalon teacher, describes his transition to Avalon from a traditional teaching environment.

I am doing a ridiculous thing today, but I think it serves a point. The ridiculous thing I am doing is sitting in my advisory and writing this chapter. I should be, what, doing anything other than this, any time other than now, because I should focus on the children, always the children, and writing books ought to happen some other time.

For example, shouldn't writing a chapter happen in the summer? As a teacher, I have summers "off", right? Or maybe I should write early in the morning, late at night, dribs and drabs in a coffee shop.

But here's the point – I write the chapter (or at least the beginning of it) in the midst of what I do because everything in a school is happening in the middle of something else. For us, according to John Lennon, life is what happens when you're busy making other plans.

When I came to Avalon School five years ago, I had missed out on the party. All the busy-ness business of startup and the insanity of the first year, coupled with the horrors of September 11 – that All happened to other people.

So, when I sit down to think about a book chapter of meaningful stuff about starting a school written by someone who never started a school, well, I feel maybe more than slightly like a professor I have who has never been a school leader teaching me about school leadership.

When you start a school, the daily emergencies obscure the tasks probably so important to the actual running of the school – or, at least, people have told me as much! Therefore, this chapter is an outsider's view about some key ways to think through starting an EdVisions school in its first few years.

I think about this through relationships – relationships you as a new staff member will have with students, staff, and parents. If you think about the concrete things that have to get done to run your school through the lens of relationships, I think it helps prioritize things. It certainly helped me to adjust from teaching for six years in traditional public schools.

Students

Since I have written these paragraphs, I have added Matt to my World Cinema seminar, printed out some math for Ben, encouraged Mike to get started on a sleep disorders project, and talked briefly with Molly about whether an open house could count as part of her senior project. In other words, if you're following the EdVisions model, you work with numerous students All the time and discuss a wide range of things.

When I worked in traditional schools, periods, desks/tables, and classroom expectations regulated contact time. A certain discipline (in my case, Language Arts) dictated my interactions with students. I knew students as Language Arts students and focused on developing their skills as readers, writers, listeners, and speakers. Students in specific lost out to the discipline of Language Arts in general.

Avalon appeared to me as a nirvana by comparison because I thought the school – as a place for independent life-long learners– would be a place where I could truly serve as a guide and cheerleader for students passionate about learning. In fact,

Avalon's current tagline boasts "Passion for Learning." Yet, once I got to Avalon, I learned (often very slowly) that students wanted to be independent life-long learners but didn't necessarily know how. In my consulting experience, I have talked with schools that ask, "How can students do projects when their skills are so low?" I found myself asking the same question.

I knew teaching as seat time and contact time and focused time. Now I watched students be independently lazy (or, if generously, habitually unfocused). As they flailed about and failed to meet deadlines, I kept wondering, "Where are the real Avalon students I read about in the pamphlet?"

If I have a first thing worth underlining in this chapter, it follows here: the project of an EdVisions school is to help students become independent life-long learners. There, I underlined it for you. Independent life-long learning is the goal (or at least one of the main goals). If you see their learning as a process that moves towards that, then you can learn as an educator in an EdVisions school to structure activities when necessary and when to let them go, when to help guide them and when to step in and demand a thing or two. You know what the end goal is supposed to be (if you buy into the EdVisions Design Essentials, which I hope you do; otherwise, this whole thing – my writing this and you reading this – wastes your time).

As one of my editors notes, how do you know you've succeeded if the goal is to help students become life-long learners: can you wait until they're dead? How we measure success in a project-based school like Avalon is perhaps impossible. In a nod to the obsession with data, EdVisions designed a study to measure students' hope, hoping to help the world of metricians understand that raising hope demonstrates success. Will that pig fly for the politicians and the metricians? Probably not in this lifetime.

Another Thing About Students

If it was all about independent life-long learning, students could really work in separate cubicles with their headphones on. More important than the work and these life-long goals is building community. Now, maybe you've heard that building community needs to be intentional, that everyone needs to be on the same page, that you need to hire like-minded people or start the school with like-minded people, but All of that really feels nebulous to me. In sum, as an editor friend points out, people need to recognize that we need community, must have it to make a small school like Avalon work.

If you want to have a community in which students actually learn to learn independently, they have to believe that their learning matters. For their learning to matter, they have to have a voice and a choice. Walter talks somewhere else about the rights and responsibilities of a student in an EdVisions school.

You see, at Avalon, Carrie worked on a Civics project with students whereby they wrote their own constitution for the school. They started along the process of becoming independent learners by being in a situation from the beginning that valued their voice in an authentic way. Their work was the real work of taking responsibility for their school.

So, through Congress and weekly circle discussions and peer mediation, students learned that their opinions mattered. Did they matter in that they were legally responsible for everything needed/required for running a school? No, they mattered insofar as they understood that their opinions could be part of the process for making decisions in the school. Some students will tell you today and tell you quite crankily that they are told up and down how much voice they have but that the school still calls the shots. That, at the end of the day, is very true. That's the running of the school.

However, if the students do not feel like anything they want or need matters, then their work suffers because of it. Their work becomes as meaningless as it might in other, less responsive settings.

How do you then keep students invested even when the staff roundly rejects some of their more outlandish or impractical ideas? You work with them to help them be accountable to others. By valuing the circle process with a talking piece (see details elsewhere) and using peer mediation to resolve student to student and student to staff (and staff to staff!) conflict, students understand that, while their role differs from that of a staff member, their involvement bolsters a school's community.

When they see and hear staff encouraging them to solve their own problems, students stop relying on staff to navigate through the school and the school experience. They recognize staff for what they are: resources.

Therefore, the second big thing to underline: independent life-long learning develops in a community when voices speak and members listen.

Parents

I have been dragging my feet on this one, no doubt about it. Right now, I tread water in the midst of a legal battle with some parents, so my thoughts are mostly glum and cynical. While those feelings lurk throughout this section, I will try to explain my journey in my evolving relationships with parents.

When I first started teaching, I feared parents. I only saw them twice or three times a year at conferences. Sometimes, I talked on the phone, but the phone never felt comfortable. I had been given great advice about making positive calls home every day and how that could build good relationships with parents (it is much better, when you have to break bad news, to already have a good relationship in which to do it), but I barely followed that advice.

At conferences, I was so scared that I did what I usually do when I'm scared: I got right up from my chair every time a parent or parents walked in and shook their hands: a sort of pre-emptive strike of niceness. I can't say whether or not the parents liked it, but the principal did and I took that as a good sign.

When I moved out to Connecticut into a high-powered suburb, the parents' time and money meant more involvement. They wrote letters to the principal, either praising or criticizing my alleged impact on their child. If they worried, parents rarely spoke to me: they went right to the top. I saw one first-year teacher get eaten alive by aggressive parents who never bothered to talk to her; by heading to the "boss", the parents wrecked her relationship with the principal because that was the news he was getting and the news wasn't good.

So, while I feared this aggressive parenting, I decided to do what I had done in my first job: meet the challenge head on. If parents complained to the principal or the department chair, I asked for a meeting with them and with the parents. I thought meeting would solve All problems, and usually my offer disarmed some parents and certainly pleased my superiors because it looked like I thought I could handle whatever problems came my way.

As you can see, I thought of my interactions with parents as always being about and around problems. Since I never called about the good news, they rarely called about it either (except for the few sweet moments of recognition, mailed to the principal).

When I came to Avalon, I assumed that the same relationship dynamic would continue: parents would always present themselves as a problem or obstacle that I needed to meet with them directly and try to discuss the problem.

I was wrong.

For one thing, Avalon was and is a very open place. People come and go when they like, and, while we have a visitor policy, parents commonly and informally dropped in, eager to get updates about their child's progress or to offer to help (either their child, the school, or both). It starts with the picnic in August where families meet one another and the staff, continues on with the August goal-setting conferences, and then carries through the year with email, phone calls, conferences, drop-ins, and the occasional observation.

At the other schools where I worked, I saw at least one hundred students a day, if not more, but at Avalon, I work with approximately 18-19 students in my advisory. While I work with other students in math, seminars, and other projects, my main focus is those 18-19 students.

While my aversion to using the phone continues, email helps me stay in contact with families. That said, I have had to learn how to manage email as well as the larger consequences of such an open and small school. As my editor friend has noted, though, email communication is a sticky wicket rife with opportunities for misinterpretation, so what to do? With email, keep it brief, stick to facts, and call meetings when possible (and bcc other key staff to keep others in the loop). What else? Review the practical stuff I think you can use:

Set Boundaries

Ok, I know I am terrible at this, but the most successful advisors I have seen at Avalon set boundaries in terms of parent contact. They have a sample voicemail message that gives a sense of how often they check their messages (once a day), when, and when they can most likely get back to the person calling (usually a day).

I of course am constantly checking email and phone messages, trying to respond immediately, but I know that this not only keeps me from working with students; it also creates an expectation with families that I can and will respond to them immediately. Very unwise.

With email, like with voicemail, set some limits. This requires working out with your staff how you use email and how to avoid letting email use you. If your staff uses email to communicate emergencies, then you face the sad reality of continua ly checking your email and scanning for the next emergency. I would recommend not using email that way.

You will have a harder time managing parent interactions if you have an open school and encourage parent access and involvement. Some parents you will see every day, and this can be good and it can be bad.

The upside, at least for me: I have stopped being afraid of and adversarial towards parents. By seeing them often, I have gotten to know them as people, as parents, and as part of their and the school's family. Parents have volunteered to work with me on theatre productions and have taken the lead in fundraising. Their access increases their commitment, and it helps me to partner with them to educate their child. It feels the way I have always wanted to work with parents: as partners.

The downside: some parents do not necessarily want to be partners. Either their excessive absence or presence makes for difficult relationships, especially in building that partnership to educate the child. So, for those parents I never see, I have to make a commitment to calling (email usually does not cut it, and it is generally unwise and the sign of middle-class privilege to assume everyone has email and internet access) and checking in with absent parents. I still struggle with this, whether I have 150 students or 18, but I know it is critical in helping a student be successful.

For parents I see all the time, I need to make sure that I try to aggressively influence how those interactions go. That is not easy, and what it mostly means is controlling how I react to the daily check-in and/or interrogation. I remind myself that parents often at the school have the time, resources, and concern for their child's learning. If I keep that in mind, I can listen more, talk less, and, when needed, politely remind visiting parents that I have X, Y, or Z to do in a moment. Of course, it could very well be that the parents lurk in the school space because they can trust you about as far as they can throw you. Some parents have 'discovered' Avalon because other schools have been less accommodating; they hope for more when they meet you.

With parents who express concerns, I still fall back on the "let's meet" model to resolve all problems, but multiple conferences end up happening for every concerned family. I strive to save conferences for our school's scheduled conference times, and, if I need an extra conference or two, I try to schedule them discreetly and efficiently within my schedule so as to not give everyone the notion that "open office hours" occur every single day and at the whim of the concerned parent.

Parents will care and will want to be involved. It is important to make sure through the setting of boundaries that you encourage their involvement in a way that does not disrupt the work of students and staff at the school. That is a good rule of thumb, so I am going to go back and underline it.

Keep Interactions Focused

Don't get me wrong -- I think informal check-ins with parents, sometimes even about subjects not immediately or directly connected to their child's learning, build and maintain your community. Yet, when you have interactions with parents that focus on their child's learning, I would recommend listening and listening and listening.

When I started out in teaching and when I am nervous, I think that, when talking with people, I need to come up with solutions right and quick, but the way to connect with parents must mirror the way we connect with students at Avalon. They need to have voice, need to express their needs, and perhaps even need to solve their own problems. If I sit back and listen, the parents usually talk themselves to where they want to go and how they plan to do it.

This doesn't always work. Some parents see a visit as a kind of performance review and duty assignment: do this, do this, do this, etc. We could spend a whole book talking about how inappropriate this is, but everyone I have been talking to recommends just listening and taking it All in without making promises and without getting defensive. Now there's some daily meditation material: one, I will not promise to do something that I do not think I should do; two, I will listen to criticism and suggestion, and not confuse either with orders. Those two might help.

Do Not Give Up (Right Away)

When families make the transition to Avalon, they still expect Avalon to look much like the past school and/or the schools of their past. As you as an educator have had to realize that you are no longer in Kansas, remember that the same realization is a tough one for families. What do they (meaning the students) do All day? – is a common question. A common comment? My child does better with structure. And yet, here at Avalon, they work in a rather open and unstructured place that requires students to take charge of their own learning.

The transition can pain families if the student does not transition in ways that demonstrate clear-cut success to parents. A lack of credits, poor grades in math and seminars, and few completed projects usually lead to claims of "this isn't working."

All of the Avalon staff have reminded me that it takes time and sometimes having that frank conversation with parents can help everyone establish some clear expectations. Help families understand the following:

Students struggle to make the transition to Avalon if they have been in traditional systems that have not been concerned with their input. Students think, through that lens, that an open environment resembles an unsupervised study ha l and act accordingly. They wait for bells and whistles and detentions and plenty of assignments. When none of those materialize, the students will act like something out of Lord of the Flies, running wild and destroying themselves and others.

Struggle for students is a good thing. Parents may expect to see immediate success, but learning to become an independent learner takes not only time but a good measure of failure. And this kind of learning can be tough because students are only running up against themselves in a school like Avalon. Their success becomes primarily what they put into it (vs. how well they play by someone else's rules). Put another way, students become successful over time at Avalon by creating their own rules. As a critical side note, my editor friend notes that I have been talking so much about independent learning while also stressing the need for community, so perhaps a better word would be "interdependent" to describe what we are trying to help students become.

That struggle can take a year or two years! Are families willing to accept that high school might take five years? If not, is summer school on the table? Slow starts in the freshman and sophomore year lead to a frenetic pace in the junior and senior years. It can be done and is done, but it requires patience. To paraphrase one Avalon student, once students know what the purpose of their education, they seek it with more energy and enthusiasm than they had before when they were just Fulfilling requirements on their way towards graduation. Only when students see graduation as a means and not an end does their education truly become theirs.

Advisors are not police officers. Advisors advise. This means that, while advisors make suggestions and offer questions and alternatives, the ultimate solutions for student problems must come from the student (except of course in cases that threaten the health and safety of students and staff in the school). Students must fo low rules at Avalon, but the most important "rule" is that students must be in charge of their learning, even if it means that they fail.

If you share these things with parents and if you remember as an advisor not to give up when students do not take the responsibility that comes with the freedom of being at Avalon, you can help foster an environment of patience that a lows the student to come to learning. As the Zen saying goes, when the student is ready, the teacher will appear.

Staff

I'm sitting here listening to the Cubs blow another lead with a combination of inept base running and pedestrian relief pitching. As the announcer notes, it doesn't matter who puts on a Cubs jersey: they always have been terrible base runners. It causes more than a little wincing because it is more than a little true.

Don't worry – I'm not just bringing up the Cubs because it's Spring Break with its attendant rare pleasure to listen to a day baseball game in the middle of the week. Instead, I focus on the concept of staff culture and how, while some baseball commentators will chalk it All up to a curse, there is a culture of losing for the Cubs. Everyone knows them to be losers. A Cub is a metaphor for losing.

Listen – the manager makes a questionable bullpen call. The catcher can't handle a pitch. The runners on first and second advance to second and third. The catcher can't handle the next pitch. The runner on third scores. The batter who went to first on ball four runs to second while the catcher spaces out at home plate with the ball in his hand. Reds 3 Cubs 2. Runners on second and third, again.

You'd just never hear the Twins play like this. But think about it. Many of the Twins came up through their farm system. They learned to play with the Twins philosophy: solid fundamentals. The Cubs, full of expensive free agents, do not have a philosophy or at least not a discernible one.

When I came to Avalon, it became clear that I had to contend with a philosophy towards education whereas in All the previous systems of which I had been a part, I might as well have been a free agent playing for the Cubs.

At Avalon, I had to understand that we were not teachers but advisors in a co-op with no principal, committed to project- based learning. What did All of this mean? From the beginning, as I think it is clear by now, I struggled to adjust. In the past, I had committed myself to notions of seat time and classroom control, notions no longer applicable.

Before Avalon, I looked upon my fellow co leagues as being at times the a lies, the adversaries, and the anonymous. Most a lies were teachers hired at the same time I was, so we went through the experience together of assimilation into a particular school. We had to contend with several levels of school politics: intradepartmental, interdepartmental, intra-school, inter-school, and district. Everywhere I went, I experienced these manifestations of politics and approached each situation mostly trying to figure out how I could teach what I wanted how I wanted (When I wanted would always be at the mercy of the schedule!).

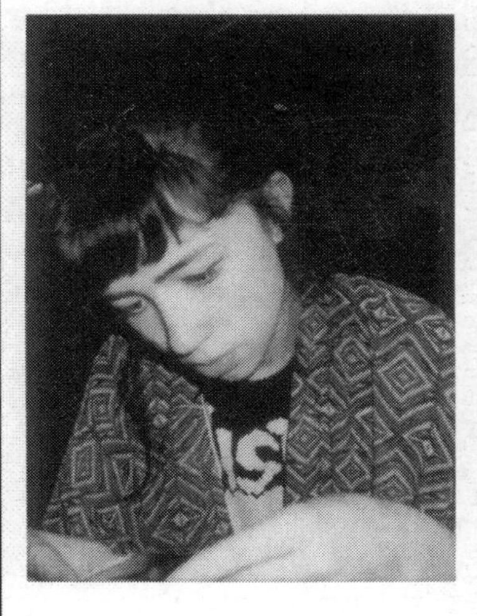

To that end, I succeeded. Often, I could teach the way I wanted and sometimes that included teaming or planning with other teachers. It could be fun and Fulfilling but never essential.

After six years of teaching, I started to feel so mercenary, so disconnected from co leagues and school buildings and district initiatives. None of it particularly mattered, but I wanted it to matter. Doing my own thing, I began to realize, did not necessarily guarantee any student an excellent education, and, to my surprise, I cared about students getting an overall education.

Therefore, I joined Avalon at the right time because I wanted to work with co leagues to create an environment for the overall education of a student. Still, I don't think I realized that. I came to Avalon with the same set of internalized and ossified attitudes, seeing colleagues as people to maybe work with and maybe not.

In a small school like Avalon, such ambivalence could not last, not by a long shot. Because our school needed to be run by the entire staff, that meant I had to work with others immediately and essentially. I worked with others to order standardized tests, develop a job evaluation rubric, and facilitate staff meetings. Once the job expectations required a commitment towards co- operative work, then I had to by nature of my work I change my attitude towards working with others.

As I try to tell people, I came to Avalon because I had imagined that, with such an open environment in such a small school, I would have the freedom to do what I wanted, but I love being at Avalon now because of the community. The community includes students and parents, of course, but the core of the community is the staff. I articulate part of the staff's philosophy that I have gleaned in five years as:

When in doubt, always check in with at least one other staff member. Without a clear principal or superior, I erroneously saw myself as the first and last line of defense in any crisis that I directly faced. Instead, we always work together. Advisors have an advisor partner who has his/her advisory right next to the advisor. By working so closely and directly with someone else, I was welcomed into the Avalon system and saw how each day and each situation required improvisation and, more importantly, collaboration. We invented our procedures because we invested in the school. I understood the charm and the challenge of working in a new school – we made it up as we went along, but we made it up together.

If you are excited about something, do something about it. Moments of leadership are ever-present at Avalon, and anyone can tackle anything: technology, personnel, standards, or what have you. When I started to understand that, as a staff member, I had to take responsibility for my own professional development as well as pitch in wherever and whenever needed, I became both anxious and exhilarated – anxious, because I had never been ultimately responsible for both myself and the school; exhilarated, because I knew that any observation or complaint I had could and should turn into me trying to find ways to work with staff to solve the problem. In this way, I did not need to accept "the way things are done."

Being a part of a co-op means relying on the staff to work together co-operatively to address concerns and solve problems. We All must work together, talk out ideas, hear other points of view, and try to get a sense of not only what the staff wants to do but also what makes sense in relation to our philosophy as a school. It means and meant that from time to time someone has to and had to speak up against the general flow towards a decision to ask: "How does this decision reflect our mission and vision? Is this what we are about?"

So, as Uncle Ben says in "Spider-Man," with great power comes great responsibility. As students and their families go through a journey in making the transition to Avalon and project-based learning, so do staff. We have to leave behind some of thingswe have learned and modify some values and views that remain. The Cubs lost today 5-2, but we don't have to claim the Cubs' culture as our own.

Final Thought

If we think of the school as our project and democratic community that inspires active learning as both our process and our product, then we can make the transition into a school like Avalon. With every project, we must be active voices in setting the parameters of our study as well as our evaluation. We cannot wait for others to pave the way for us, tell us what to do, or write the book that answers All the questions. We must model the life-long learning we wish our students to do. As Gandhi said, we must be the change we wish to see in the world. If this chapter does anything, I hope it helps anyone interested in starting a project-based school like Avalon to see, to know, and to understand that only through a lowing yourself and others to learn can you succeed.

Chapter 5

Voices of Students and Parents

Ron Newell weaves together interviews of students and parents from several project-based schools to give a picture of the student experience at Avalon.

The secret of education lies in respecting the pupil. It is not for you to choose what he shall know, what he shall do. It is chosen and foreordained, and only he holds the key to his own secret.

- Ralph Waldo Emerson

Lynn Stoddard, in his book Educating for Human Greatness, explains that there are three inherent core drives within each human:

- The drive to be a recognized "somebody" (Identity). This drive is much more than the need to merely survive or exist. It is an intense need of the human spirit to fulfill one's unique potential as a special contributor to the world. It is a need to count for something, to have a sense of self-worth. It is a drive to answer the questions, who am I? Why do I exist? And what is the purpose of my life? It is a never-ending quest for Identity.

- The drive for warm human relationships (Interaction). This drive confirms another well-known characteristic of human nature- we are All born with a need to love and be loved. Everyone feels a deep need to belong and have a sense of community with other human beings. We have a built-in need to communicate with others. This is the second most powerful motivating force of human nature. It is the force of Interaction.

- The drive for truth and knowledge (Inquiry), Human beings are born curious. They are born with a strong drive to make sense of the world and to acquire personal knowledge and wisdom. Curiosity is the third most powerful motivating force of human nature. It is the force of personal Inquiry (Stoddard 2003, p. 27-28).

Stoddard (2003) goes on to say, "If these innate drives are universal, as it appears they are, it means we can hold children responsible for their own learning and development. Everyone is designed for greatness" (p. 28).

As a result of the recognition of these truths, Stoddard came to the conclusion that the school curriculum has become the end, not the means, of schooling and learning. Parents and children seek identity, interaction, and inquiry, not canned lessons, time- based courses, and Carnegie units. We at EdVisions know this to be true. When we visit the schools founded on the personalized project-based approach, we continually hear similar responses. This chapter is a compilation of the voices of students and parents expressing the effects of these "cool schools." Listen to these voices and see that Stoddard's observations ring true.

Among the comments from students and parents, you will see a number of attributes expressed: a sense of community, the freedom and responsibility fostered by the learning program, and the feeling students have for each other and for their advisor and teachers. All of those bespeak of valuing identity, interaction, and inquiry. The comments are divided by the three categories Stoddard mentions as being most important in a student's education. We will begin with a sense of identity.

Identity

When students were asked what element of their schools determined it to be a "cool school," most identified freedom. But freedom comes in many guises, one of them being a lowed to be your own individual. "I can go to school being bold about my beliefs and who I am," said one student. Another indicated his school "lets you be you," another "this is a great school because the students get to be themselves." Several commented that it was not only their individual freedom, but "a l the students at this school are so free in personality. Also they don't really care what anyone thinks about them." This means that peer pressures that cause many problems in large schools are no longer menacing. When individuals are a lowed free expression, there is less negative talk.

As others put it, "You can be yourself and not care what others have to say." Another's expression: "Everyone has their own personality and their unique ideas. This school has its own perspective for each individual. I am only a freshman here and I already have set goals for my future." Another student described their school as cool because "there are a lot of very interesting people at this school" and "there is a mix of different personalities at this school."

Parents echoed these comments about identity: "What a wonderful opportunity you have given us-a school where the kids don't fit a stereotype and the teachers care about everyone" and "The change has been great for my son. I feel that my son is appreciated for who he is."

One student sums it up by stating, "At other schools we were treated like we were little kids and here we are treated more like adults and that makes me feel safer and it makes me feel like I can do more."

Another aspect of identity is demonstrated by teachers who "treat each student individually-it is great quality for a school to have. Students need that kind of attention." Teachers deal with students in a totally different capacity - one of advisor and facilitators rather than as directive authoritarians. Consequently, as another student remarked, "We get to have personal relationships with our teachers." Additional comments validating the importance of identity are "You get more one-on-one learning," and "You also have more of a friendly relationship with your advisor and teachers. The teachers understand problems that students have and instead of telling them to deal with it, they take the time to talk to the student about the problem and help with ways to solve it or make the situation better."

Also, the schools exhibit valuing student identity by a lowing students choice in the learning program. Because the schools are primarily about self-directed learning, each student chooses the content of their projects from their interests. Rather than curriculum driven, the projects are authentic and realistic to the students. From this process, students "learn more responsibility because they aren't being told what to do, they're set free." Additional comments were made regarding freedom to choose the manner of learning: "As a student you have a say in what goes on." "I can learn about whatever I want to learn about and I can get credit for projects in the summer and at home." "I get to plan my day rather than have someone else plan it for me." "I can study what I want. There are no required classes where I have to listen to a teacher lecture. There is a lot more independence, -which I appreciate very much." "It gives us a chance to learn the things that we actually want to learn." "I get to learn more stuff I need for future careers." "We have the opportunity to do things differently."

Not only do students have the choice of subject matter and study time, but they learn to be responsible as a result of the project process. "It is up to you to get your own education or not," exclaims one student. "You get to make or break your education-it is in your hands," said another. Because "it is more on you to get your work done," students feel valued for their contributions.

Another aspect of identity is the fact that students may work at an individual pace and not be captive to the time-based curriculum. "It has helped me be more responsible and a lows me to work on my own schedule," said one student. "You can take your time and not feel rushed," said another. "I am more successful at this school than my other school because I am working at my own pace and I don't have to stop at a certain time and switch subjects." "We don't have homework unless we want to," said one student. "We can choose our own projects, and you don't have to go from class to class and learn about boring subjects." One student said, "We have more individual rights and we can work at our own pace," thereby linking rights to decisions about timeliness of learning. Having the rights to work at an individual pace is so powerful that one student said, "I wake up and want to go to school because you can work at your own pace." Another said, "The fact that I am in control of my future and of what I want to learn keeps me motivated to continue working." Following are additional powerful statements:

"This school is different from other schools because we don't just sit around in a classroom and listen to what teachers are saying and then be expected to memorize it all and take a test. Here we're given a chance to learn what we want and make a product we want. I don't know about other students here, but that really makes a difference!"

"Advisors will guide you on what you need to do when a teacher will tell you what you have to do. The choices we make become the outcome for daily life. I like the independence.

I think that if a student can work independently that they can achieve anything, they can accomplish anything they want. When I was in the normal school I didn't know what I wanted to do. Now I am interested in computer technology, networking, and other things. I really like the opportunities at this school."

"I think the thing I would miss the most, were I to switch schools, would be not needing permission to do things such as use the bathroom or get a drink of water. If, at a high school level, we are expected to make decisions that will affect our whole lives, say choosing a college, why can't we pee without permission?"

"I love being able to work on projects that interest me and keep me wanting to learn more about everything. I feel sorry for people who are not able to do what they want and learn about things they find fascinating."

Being acknowledged for having a separate identity certainly can be a strong motivator. A strong sense of identity leads to self- efficacy and success. "I am more successful at this school because I will be studying what I need to learn for what I want to become."

When a student said, "I can be who I am," they speak for All students of EdVisions schools. Their identities matter. They do not have to become automatons and one of the anonymous dots in the middle of the be l curve.

Interaction

The theme of freedom is expressed in many of the comments. This is certainly true for the concept of interaction. EdVisions schools are inherently choice ridden and democratic as a result of being organized around small-group advisories, individual and small-group projects, group assessments, and place-based learning. In addition, they are organized around student- directed projects, not classes. Students determine their schedules according to their learning activities, not around what teachers design.

Advisories are usually in a ratio of 1 to 18, and school sizes are generally 100 to 150 students. This small size a lows for more interaction between advisors and students, students and students, and advisors and parents. Not only is identity valued, but so is the interaction of student to student, student to advisor, and student to community. Students therefore express themselves more freely, make decisions more often, and experience more verbal interaction than in traditional schools. Some of the comments pertaining to the freedom a lowed students include the following:

"I think that learning in an environment that allows freedom can give a person choices that they would not have in a 'normal' school."

"This school is a good helpful way to learn and study different subjects the way you want to learn them, and I think that is the best way to learn." "Because I can choose what I want to do; the school does not choose what I have to do."

"To have freedom is what everyone (kid and adult) is looking for, and I think to have that makes school so much better and I actually look forward to going to school."

"You have more freedom to do what you are really interested in through your projects."

"[This school] opens opportunities you would never think of. It gives you more of an independent learning basis which helps you lead your life as an independent person. It also shows a lot more career opportunities and broadens your horizons. The best thing is the free will, because you have a choice in what you do and not just your subject to do what 'the teacher knows is best."

This concept of free will is not only about identity but also about interactions a lowed by the school setting. When a school establishes a routine for the purpose of setting students free to choose, a new dynamic creates new relationships between teachers and students. Students choose the content and the time of their learning, and teachers become advisors rather than deliverers of content. This freedom a lows students to create both their own learning time and space:

"By far my favorite aspect of this school is the independence students get. In attending a project-based school, I have the freedom to study what I want when I want to. For instance, this morning, at the end of math class, I was just learning something new and I didn't want to stop so I didn't. I continued working on math for the next hour, too. Not only do I have the freedom to manage my own time here, but I also have the freedom to study what I want."

But simply having the time to learn what they want can be daunting. Some students recognized that they had to accept the responsibility to use their time wisely:

"[This school] has a lot more freedom but you have to be really responsible and don't abuse it or you'll get behind and it's hard to catch up." "For one thing, I enjoy the freedom that I have here. I can learn about the things that I want to learn about. Of course, with freedom comes responsibility and at times, it is difficult to get everything done and stay on task all of the time."

"On the other hand, the worst thing about going to [this school] would also have to be the freedom that I have.

The downside to freedom is the responsibility. It was not terribly difficult for me to come to [this school] because I am a responsible person. However, I have seen many people who took advantage of the freedom they received and never did anything school related. Being responsible for your own education is something most people don't even think about until they're in college. Having that responsibility at a younger age than most is sometimes difficult for me because it adds a little bit of extra stress around school. Overall though, I enjoy being responsible and having freedom in my education. I feel prepared to go to college and learn what I want to know so I can become the person I want to be."

Students concluding wise use of time attests to the fact that they have learned to become self-directed learners. That is why these schools are constructed the way they are and why the interactions are built on individual student needs, not on teacher needs. In a lowing freedom for students to choose content, a distinct interaction occurs.

The primary interaction, however, is the way the schools value the adolescent need for acceptance and community. The feeling of acceptance was a frequent response made by students. "It is a small school and I just love small schools because then you know just about everyone," remarked one student. Another student said, "I also like how most of the students get along and everybody knows everybody." A large part of this acceptance is evidence of caring and the lack of bullying: "There are not any cliques at [this school]," said one student; "I enjoy this school because I don't have to put up with bullies," exclaimed another. "You could get picked on during normal school but not much here," remarked another student. Another student was more inclusive: "This school is nice. At my other schools there was a lot of fighting, cussing and the teachers were mean. Here there is no fighting and the teachers are better."

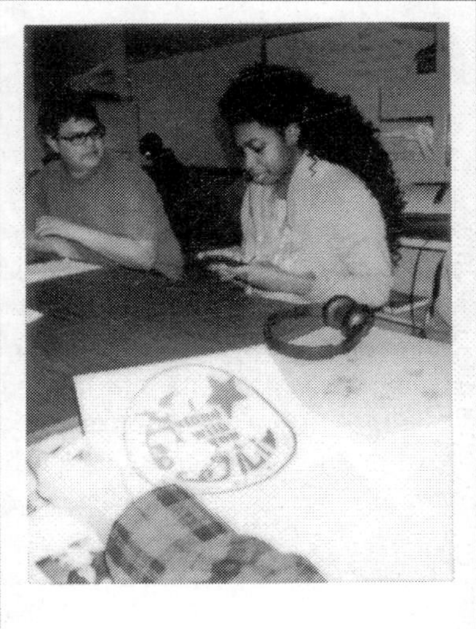

The small communities and caring atmospheres lead to development of friendships: "I have awesome friends in this small school. I know so many people, and I get along with a lot of them," said one student. "Everyone is very nice arid I'm just about friends with everyone," said another." Some reacted to the non-graded programs: "I also like how most of the students get along and everybody knows everybody. It gives the younger students a chance to interact with older students and vice versa." Another student had this to say: "There are no grades, and we All work together. I mean a sixteen-year-old and a thirteen-year- old can do a project together without feeling weird." These friendships extend beyond just being pals. It also refers to friendships made between students and advisors: one student refers to an advisor as "my friend-for the last couple of weeks we have been best of friends."

Many students referred to the small atmosphere created by the learning communities in more general terms: "I think this is the greatest school be- cause of the atmosphere and the people in it. All the kids and advisors are so nice and easy to talk to. Everyone is so friendly and thoughtful." And yet another remarked, "You will pretty much know everyone you go to school with and will have better interaction with the teacher." One student said, "[This school] is the coolest school in America because everyone there is nice and we All get along."

Others noted the small size of groups or classes had benefits: "This is a good school if you have a hard time learning in big groups. The teachers have smaller classes than most public schools, so they can work with you more one on one." With smaller groupings, "the staff can pay more attention to each kid." Another remarked, "I also like how when you ask a question here the teacher has time to explain it because there is a better student-to-teacher ratio."

With the smaller ratios of students to teacher, "if you need help the teacher will give you help, and you will learn it instead of never understanding your work." Another student said, "If you are having a hard time understanding something, you get the one-an-one help you need." By having this one-on-one help, "advisors help you do better." Two students referred to the difference between the small EdVisions learning community and a previous school: "I can get more help than last year," said one.

"This school is a lot different from the last one I attended because it is smaller so the teachers actually get a chance to help the students with their work when they need it," exclaimed another. One student referred to help coming from not only the advisors: "Whether it is between students or a student and a teacher, there will always be several people willing to help you."

The small communities lead to a feeling of safety: "With the small amount of people, I feel like I can concentrate more," said one student. Another said that "the environment is different here. It just feels a lot safer." And there were comments from students noting the family-like atmosphere of their schools: "Our school doesn't seem like much if you just look at the building, but if you come inside and join our school it's like we are one big happy family." Another student recognized that the small atmosphere leads to more inclusion of family: "I also think that [this school] is cool because the teachers get to know your family where in a larger school the only thing you know about that teacher is his or her last name." The small, caring, family-like atmosphere leads to better results for students.

Many students referred to their teacher and advisors as being caring and concerned about them: "I like this school because the teachers are nice", said one. "There are friends and teachers who care about you and also the kids here look out for one another, and are good people," remarked an- other. "The other schools I attended were huge and the teachers didn't have time for you," said another. Probably the most telling comment was, "Instead of a nagging teacher, you have advisors who help when help is needed. That takes some of the pressure off and you can learn and accomplish more." Another powerful statement:

"We don't have teachers constantly making us feel like we're in a hurry to get stuff done when we can choose how much time we want to spend on it. I think it is a good thing that these teachers finally got sick of pushing kids around and decided that there's a different way to learn. Old school teachers are just teaching kids not to be independent. They constantly tell the kids what to do, where to go and when to get there. They don't let the kids speak for themselves. They shouldn't like teaching like that."

It appears the students clearly understand the difference between an adviser and a traditional schoolteacher. Two other comments bear that out: "There are teachers here who really believe in what they are doing. They are willing to help us as students to succeed. They will take their time to make sure you understand something" and "The teachers really seem to care about you, they are more like friends than big mean grumpy teachers. I do believe that having an advisor makes your feelings be more understood." Because of the small school size, the advisory system, and small groupings, each individual student receives the help he or she needs to succeed.

The primary point of interaction is to develop a sense of trust and respect for our fellow man. Some of the student comments were quite mature in recognizing the effect of positive interactions: "The students are respectful and the teachers help us to the best of their abilities," said one student. Another student recognized that "it is a relaxed environment and even if you make a fool of yourself, everyone still loves you." Another said, "In this school people accept me for who I am." Another comment was, "Everyone is so polite."

These students are recognizing that the interactions incurred in the Ed-Visions learning communities are respectful, positive, affirming, and caring. This respect for the individual (identity) and the allowance of interaction contribute to the creation of students who become respectful and caring citizens. As a student said, "Later in life, the students who attended [this school] will know how important it is to treat others with respect, and treat each point of view equally. The world these days needs more people like that."

The previous comments exhibit a strong declaration for these types of small-school environments. There are too few school settings in which the students perceive their advisor and teacher as their friend and advocate, that induce the feeling of family, or that help develop trust and respect for each other. For the students to react with such strong sentiments of acceptance, friendship, trust, respect, and camaraderie is indeed heartwarming.

Inquiry

The primary point made by student comments, again, had to do with freedom, in this case freedom to pursue an interest. Inquiry is a powerful tool for learning when a student is self-directed and therefore intrinsically motivated. From the large number of statements received regarding freedom of choice, some of the most powerful statements had to do with discovery: "I can explore areas I am interested in," said one student. "You can study or do a project on just about anything you're interested in" and "I like the fact we get to choose what we would like to learn about" are two other relevant comments.

Students were more reflective about learning than they were about interaction and identity:

"[l like] the freedom we have to walk around and not feel confined to a classroom, the freedom to study what we want to learn and be able to use the information and expand on it and not have to go on to the next subject, and the freedom to go out into the community and learn from other people who already are experts in the field we are studying at the time."

"I have the freedom here to explore in all different directions - something most schools don't have. I can spend all day working on one project if I want to, or I can work on seven projects in a day."

"Projects can be fun and involve things that you actually enjoy. Instead of doing boring homework about things you don't care about and that you'll just forget after a test, you can do projects that are enjoyable and things that are interesting. The more something fits your individual interests the more likely you'll remember it and you will more likely work harder at completing it. At [this] school you will learn things that you will use for life instead of just forgetting them when you're out of school."

These statements exhibit the power of awe and wonder in learning. These students have recognized that following a teacher- driven curriculum does not result in the most effective learning. A lowing them to inquire into areas of interest led to learning more deeply and with greater motivation.

Others spoke of experiential learning:

"I agree that most learning is done through experience, and by doing activities and participating in educational things we are going to learn so much more."

"At the other school you do worksheets, and a lot of busy work. At our school you don't do busy work, you do things that you want to do and that you think are important."

"We learn in fun and exciting ways. We do hands-on learning and we do lots of fun field trips relating to core classes, or inspiring us to do projects."

"I am more successful because I think we have a lot more opportunities to get out of school and explore the world around us."

Projects are motivating for students. Because they determine their own project parameters, interest remains high and more is learned. Some related comments were the following:

"Our projects definitely deal with things we enjoy doing. My computer networking project deals with one of my possible career choices."

"The projects are good. I can choose anything that I want to learn about and do a project on it. It's a great way to learn. I can learn my own way." "The best thing is I like choosing and teaching myself what I want to learn about. I like that you get to choose what you want to do for your project, when you want it to be due, and what you want it to look like! That is the best thing here. There are many more, but that is the best."

"I like doing projects of my choice, and the projects help me to learn better."

Choice is such a powerful human need. It is when we choose to learn that we actually engage in learning. In Passion for Learning (2003), I wrote that wel earn something only when we perceive the need to learn it. These students have recognized the need to learn out of interest. From their interest they were able to deepen their study via inquiry while meeting state standards (and in many cases going beyond them).

Some students progressed beyond a mere interest; they became passionate about what they were doing:

"I had more fun doing this project than I had at Disney World when I was nine. I loved writing something that I was really passionate about, and reading about literature and parallels between stories and myths, and then thinking for a long time and trying to find a way for every bit of information that I received to fit into my thesis statement."

The previous comment was made by a fourteen-year-old. If only all ninth graders were that interested and passionate about inquiring into literature! Another comment:

"I did a project that let me do a hands-on study: my own research. In a normal class, I would have taken data from Professor Somebody-or-other's study and made conclusions based on that. Project-based learning let me do my study and create my own data. It made the project all the more relevant. I cared about what I was learning and what the final result was. The data was no longer strings of numbers crowding the page; now it was my time and energy showing something positive, an end result. It was my information, my labor, my project."

This ownership in the learning process is difficult to attain in the traditional setting. Students in the project-based schools of the EdVisions community speak with passion of their learning experiences. They recognize the extent to which they are learning. Many commented on how much more they could learn in the student- driven project-based system:

"Project-based learning is a wonderful setup. Personally, I could do well in a 'normal' setup, but I enjoy PBL much more. I am able to learn about things that would not be mentioned in a typical school, and I am not restricted by what the state says I need to know. I learn important skills like time management and public speaking, which I think are much more important than knowing when Thomas Jefferson died. A really useful tool I have used is finding resources. At [this school] there are hardly any textbooks, so we have to find information on our own. I have learned much more about finding valid sources than I ever learned before and I know that this will help me in the long run."

Another student related how lack of interest became a more in-depth interest:

"The main reason I did not like history was because there are so many things to remember, and I did not know why I had to remember them other than what my teacher told me. Now that I know how deep history is, I can see myself finding some part in history interesting and wanting to learn more about it."

By inquiring into aspects of history of interest to the student, it became possible to learn to enjoy the depth and breadth of the subject. Two other comments exhibit another sort of in-depth learning:

"I have done projects varying from art creation to political activism. I think that project-based learning is great for high school students because it provides the structure and comfort that gives a solid base to build off of, but it also supplies resources and space to explore yourself and your place in the world. Attending a school where I have been given so much responsibility and freedom has helped me become a much more self-assured and reliable person."

"Project-based learning, I feel, is one of the most in-depth ways to learn about a topic. Not only do you have to be motivated on a personal level, in order to find the means necessary to begin, go through with, and complete a project, but you have to rely on your community, both within [the school] and outside of, in order to get from beginning to end. It's a wonderful way to encourage youth to be involved, to expand their minds, and to open up to all possibilities. As much as I hate grad standards, I must admit, I love seeing the creative ways people are able to achieve them. I love learning about what other people are doing and how motivated in my own projects I become. I enjoy the freedom and responsibility that project-based learning has to offer. The fact that I can structure a project that can take 500 hours or a project that takes 30 is wonderful, giving me opportunities I would not have had otherwise."

These two students are reacting to the ways project-based learning and the spirit of inquiry lead to an understanding of yourself and your world. Inquiry expands the mind and develops persistence. The freedom to formulate your own plan, find your own resources, and produce your own product results in powerful learning ..

The students recognize the route to finished projects is not without obstacles. The passion, the awe, and the wonderment of learning are not consistently obvious. A well-rounded education comes with a price. The questioning and inquiring pedagogy, utilized at the EdVisions schools, also helps students realize the value of life skills such as determination and persistence:

"I think that project-based learning is a good thing for so many people and I really enjoy the project picking part. It just takes a lot of self-discipline, which is something that I know I have to work a little harder on."

Most students come to the conclusion at some time that project-based learning is not an easy way through high school. If they ignore the need for work and persistence, they may fail to graduate. But by coming to that realization, first by applying persistence through interests and the spirit of inquiry, they are then better equipped for the world. Another comment:

"This system is not, however, meant for everyone. It requires a lot of self-motivation. The majority of the work done during school hours is done completely separately from teachers. Students must be able to manage their time and stay on task. This has proven difficult for some students (including myself) and is, in my opinion, the flaw in the system. This possibility is rooted in independent learning, unfortunately, and could not be entirely removed without greatly compromising project-based learning. In my opinion the positive aspects of project- based learning outweigh the flaws, and it is a beneficial program for many."

This student's recognition of the need for discipline is typical of students' reflection after experiencing the EdVisions system for more than a year. The recognition of the need for self-discipline is the key to success in any endeavor. That is why it is necessary to initiate self-interests and a spirit of inquiry prior to "mandating" student learning. Regardless of students' initial thoughts, they eventually come to the same conclusion as the student quoted here:

"Coming from a traditional junior high and a brief period at a traditional high school I can honestly say that I greatly prefer the project-based learning style. Although most students may end up with a slightly-less-than- rounded four years, what they do study in that time will be learned in far greater detail due both to a student's interest and the flexibility within the topic itself. This is not to say, however, that a project-based student cannot get a rounded education; with some determination it is entirely possible to meet or even exceed the range of study provided by most schools. Our system can give a student access to areas of study rarely seen in traditional schools, especially in the arts and social sciences."

Or, as one student put it, "At my old school I wasn't learning anything. But here I am learning." That is the sum total of the power of inquiry- leading to the perception of increased understanding and learning of additional life skills that will contribute to their lifelong habits.

Many of the students stated they would not return to traditional ways of learning: "I never want to go back to the old way of being taught. I want to learn what I want to learn," said one. Others spoke of their passion for the school: "I used to count the days, hours, and seconds until that glorious day in June when I was finally free! As I sit here at [my school] I hardly care when school is over, and why is that? It is because of the freedom."

Yet others described the alternative as being daunting: "Without [this school] I would not be finishing school," said one student.

"Without [this school] I would be overwhelmed with boredom," said another. And when a student says that "without [this school] I probably would have dropped out of school by now," you know that the experience of being valued as a human being, having freedom to choose what and when to learn, and developing trust and respect via the interactions of All members of the learning community was a powerful experience.

There were some statements made by parents that spoke to the power of valuing student identity, interaction, and inquiry.

"It was like a light was turned on in our child since attending [the school]. She has grown, not just academically, but as an individual. She has become more confident, and in many ways more responsible. We think the positive relationships she has with both students and staff at [the school], and the fact that she is respected as an individual there, has done that for her."

Another parent stated that their "daughter likes school, enjoys learning through her projects, has truly grown emotionally (good friends, better self-esteem), and enjoys the classes offered by the school. We see a very helpful staff that is always friendly and willing to cope with any issue." Other comments by parents include the following:

"I have been amazed by the changes in my son's attitude and behavior throughout the year, to see how much he has progressed in such a small amount of time. I would have to say that it is due to the different teaching methods of the [school] staff, and the ideas of letting children make some decisions about their education."

"It is extremely encouraging to hear the change in our son's attitude toward learning and school! He speaks very highly of his teachers ... he is feeling challenged and encouraged by his teachers."

One parent referred to the problems her child had while attending other schools and how the present school has changed everything: "He is so happy and looks forward to going to school. He feels that he belongs at this school and he has been shown respect as an individual with talents and a mind of his own. [His] grades are above average and the changes are truly remarkable. If you were to read my son's last eight years of school history and then view my son in this school you would not believe it was the same child. The change is the most remarkable one I think you will find in this entire school. As a parent I love the fact I can walk into the classroom any time of day and sit down and see the learning process firsthand."

Another parent simply stated that the difference for her child was "there are no more tears." Imagine that going to school drives young people to tears. What does that say about a learning community? If we do nothing else, we ought to create the kinds of communities that value the joy of acceptance of self, the joy of being in a family of kindred spirits, and the joy of the wonderment of discovery. The voices of the students in the EdVisions schools speak eloquently to the fact that the Minnesota New Country School model can create such environments. In closing, a parent's comment is directed to All advisors, board members, support staff members, and All who have been involved in creating caring learning communities: "Thank you, thank you, thank you for All your hard work and creative vision!"

References

Newell, R. (2003). Passion for learning: How a project-based system meets the needs of 21st-century students. Lanham, MD: Scarecrow Press.

Stoddard, L. (2003). Educating for human greatness. Brandon, VT: Holistic Education Press.

*With contributions from advisors, students, and parents of Agriculture and Food Sciences Academy (Little Canada. MN), Avalon Charter School (St. Paul. MN), Explore Knowledge Academy (Henderson. NY), High School for the Recording Arts (St. Paul, MN), Harbor City International School (Duluth, MN), Minnesota New Country School (Henderson, MN), New Century Charter School (Hutchinson, MN), RiverBend Academy (Mankato, MNJ. and Valey New School (Appleton. WI).

Chapter 6

Constituting a Democratic Learning Community: The Avalon Experience

Walter Enloe, Carrie Bakken and Andrea Martin, with Caitlin Rude tell the story, from both student and teacher perspective, of the forming of Avalon's constitution.

We, the People of Avalon, in order to provide for a safe and productive learning environment, promote the obtaining and using of knowledge for the benefit of those around us, and ensure general happiness, do ordain and establish this constitution for Avalon high school.

-Preamble to the Avalon High School Constitution

Really we were already completely democratic before our constitution; student self-interest is central to the school - student choice is a student right and responsibility to do as well as you can, a kind of freedom when it is based upon your personal choice.

-Caitlin Rude, senior, Avalon High School

avalon High School in St. Paul was organized in 2001 by a group of parents who wanted to create a small "people-centered" postsecondary preparatory school of "outstanding character." In their search for teachers (and they attracted hundreds of inquiries), they advertised by asking, "What if teachers could design the ideal school? We can!" They were "seeking passionate, inspired, and hardworking individuals to build an imaginative, creative, and disciplined learning community." The school would be characterized by teacher ownership, collaborative teaching and decision making, highly innovative curricula, a small learning community, teacher development as a priority, and a truly supportive community.

Following the Minnesota New Country School model, Avalon became a teacher-owned school and a member of the EdVisions cooperative. Avalon became a teaming community combining a college prep focus, interdisciplinary seminars, and a strong technology component all centered on project learning and the Minnesota" graduation standards. This approach is complemented by extensive development individually and as a community in ethics and conflict resolution, interpersonal and life skills, and active citizenship and community service.

In its founding documents, Avalon states that it will "build a school culture and a set of values centered on excellence and active citizenship" and that it will "develop leadership opportunities for all participants. All members of the school community will be involved in decision making, and students will be given a real voice and stake in the school." The founders, who also created the Twin Cities Academy Middle School several years earlier, were guided by the Basic School model of Ernest Boyer and the Carnegie Foundation for the Advancement of Teaching.

Though the model was designed for early primary, the founders believed that if students had attended a Basic School through their elementary years, Avalon should be the perfect high school learning community for them because of the emphasis on strong interpersonal relationships and the virtues of democratic character, a project focus on active learning and interdisciplinary study, and a participatory learning community where students were, at the center, joined by parents as partners and teachers as leaders.

Boyer speaks to essential conditions for creating authentic, democratic learning communities. He identifies six qualities of human interaction that are vital for creating authentic learning communities where every member is known: by name, by interests, by dispositions, by unique personhood, by contributions, and by productions. An authentic learning community would be a place with these qualities: purposeful, caring, disciplined, celebrative, communicative, and just:

The basic school is, above all else, a community for learning, a place where staff and students, along with parents, have a shared vision of what the institution is seeking to accomplish. There is simply no way to achieve educational excellence in a school where purposes are blurred, where teachers and students fail to communicate thoughtfully with others, and where parents are uninvolved in the education of their children. Community is, without question, the glue that holds an effective school together. (Boyer 1995, 18)

The founders of Avalon were also influenced by the philosophy of Jean Piaget, the great theorist of human development who advocated both an activity pedagogy and collaborative learning environments where students worked together to meet both personal and collective needs. He once remarked that each classroom should have two rooms - one for the teacher and student and one for just the students who earned the right to be free from adult constraints and autonomous among peers. Piaget based many of his later ideas for school communities on the 1948 Universal Declaration of Human Rights; likewise, the founding parents wanted Avalon to be as inclusive as possible contributing to an integrative (rather than desegregated) society.

Article 26 of the declaration reads in part:

Education shall be directed toward the full development of the human personality and to the strengthening of respect for human rights and fundamental freedoms. It shall promote understanding, tolerance and friendship among all nations, racial or religious groups, and shall further the activities of the United Nations for the maintenance of peace.

In interviews with the original school founders, it is very clear that they began with a specific definition of citizenship based on the work of Harry Boyte and the Center of Democracy and Citizenship, a learning place in grassroots civic leadership. From Reinventing Citizenship: The Practice of Public Work, governance and citizenship is defined as government not simply for us but of us and by us. Nor is citizenship simply voting and volunteering, for active citizenship is foremost leadership and public problem solving by ordinary folk:

Active, public citizenship begins and is grounded in our everyday institutional environments - the places wellive and work, go to school, volunteer, participate in communities of faith. It is public-spirited and practical: not utopian or immaculate but part of the messy, difficult, give-and-take process of problem solving. Citizenship links our daily life and interests to larger public values and arenas. Through citizenship we build and exercise our power. (Boyte 1995, p. 8)

More specifically, politics is understood as citizen politics, grounded in our daily institutional environments in public work, that is, collaborative civic work that is visible and significant to its stakeholders:

Active citizenship is tied to an understanding of public life as diverse, contentious, and linked to, but distinct from, private and communal life. Thus the role of the citizen can connect people across lines of difference for the purpose of governing and problem solving, drawing on distinct cultural identities and other communities. (Boyte 1995,8)

Avalon's stated mission, that "Avalon School is a strong, nurturing community that inspires active learning, local action, and global awareness," captures the essence of the school: a school where teachers and students take ownership of their work. In the following pages, we conclude with the voices of students and teachers regarding their congress and school constitution.

Student Perspectives From Interviews and Reflection Papers

The Avalon Constitution and Congress were originally created in a block seminar called "Creating the Avalon Constitution." About twenty of us students and Carrie (Bakken, an adviser and seminar leader) thought we could do it in one block (term), but it took two blocks to complete it. It was so difficult. It was painfully put together, constituted if you will. Why? Because of all the arguments and deliberations over wording and meaning and trying to be consistent. I recently read that when the founding fathers (and mother, let's not forget Abigail Adams) knew more what each didn't want than what they wanted together, they weren't sure at the constitutional meetings what they would come up with. You can see this quite clearly in the Federalist Papers. Some wanted to limit the rights of citizens, some wanted ordinary citizens to govern, and others wanted consent of the governed through representation. This was very difficult work and it took years.

We took months.

Well, we were like that constitutional convention. At one point wellocked ourselves in a room for two days every week and deliberated. There were so many perspectives and needs 'and wants. It was amazing really. There was lots of debate about who governs, who makes decisions, who's got the power. We took the U.S. Constitution as our model.

Do we see connections between what we did and our constitution and what the original founders did and created? Well those men had little to follow-the Articles of Confederation and knowledge of the Iroquois nation's government, I believe. Our school constitution is based on the U.S. Constitution - it is the one wellive under and the constitution most familiar to us. Wellooked at other schools, but most weren't constituted with an actual constitution document, plus we have different structures and different needs. We did have the Paideia School's constitution, Walter's old school, and it was helpful to see that students could actually write a constitution. And they were younger (middle school); it is amazing to find out that constitution at Paideia is about thirty years old and has stood the test of time and has been amended, too. But we really needed our own, for we too are unique.

The Avalon Congress is open to all; usually at the weekly convening of the Congress, there is one adviser and ten to fifteen kids (about 15 percent) on a regular basis. Probably 50 to 60 percent are interested in the Congress's deliberations in some concrete way. One example of increased involvement was when maybe 30 to 40 percent of the school showed up when we were debating the pledge of allegiance in school.

Why is the Congress important? It allows student input on specific issues and general ones, too; also, everyone, including staff, can have a voice. The Congress and the constitution are really needed on a large scale (such as large schools), but on a small scale it depends on how people really get along; you don't need rules until you need them. On a small scale here at Avalon, we resolve issues one on one or with peer mediation; most issues between people are how to resolve issues and create a respectful environment.

Really we were already completely democratic before our constitution; students' self-interest is central to the school - student choice is a student right, and responsibility to do as well as you can is a kind of freedom when it is based on your personal choice. School life is not simply framed in terms of right and wrong with only one group having all the authority and power; teachers are leaders here-there isn't the hierarchy existing in traditional schools. Any member of this community can bring an issue to the school board or to teachers or to the student body. This is a trusting place where you are who you are and you can be who you want to be.

One of our strengths is peer mediation and restorative circles. Usually we somehow go through this and agree to disagree or agree to agree; most "cases" are usually where someone says something mean or stupid, not violence, and mediation "clears the air."

Our culture is being a small place organized around interpersonal relationships: good community, one on one, small groups, good relationships. But you have to work at making it a good place. It doesn't just happen. Just because you're small doesn't make you a great school. If you have a school of 500 or 1,500, you need formal structures, rules, and procedures, especially around authority, power, and status. A constitution in a school of 150 is going to be different than in a school of 2,000 because in a school of 150 everyone knows each other and you are "constituted" not by laws but by relationships between people who know, tolerate, and respect each other.

The great thing with our constitution is you can amend it; you can change the actual constitution, as school is ever changing and is a peaceful place. So we changed the judiciary - the judges had no cases. Anyway, with a judicial system you had litigation and a verdict - a poor way, really, to resolve issues.

Teacher Voices From Conversations and Interviews

Almost every person in the Constitution Seminar, in their reflection paper, responded to the fundamental question, How much power can students really have? The most contentious issue in the whole process of writing the constitution was "should the school staff (adults) have executive veto power over the Congress or legislative branch (which is open to all school members, students and staff alike)." We talked a lot about in loco parentis, that we staff were professional educators, legally responsible for students' safety and well-being. Legally, and particularly in such a litigious culture, parents trusted the staff to care for and protect students. Some students countered with "If you really trust us we should be able to make all decisions." Others understood their role as students. Though interest was shown in the school's budget and personnel practices, they were less interested in being accountable for all decisions. They needed to know they were being heard. They needed to know they had choices and could make many decisions. And that was power!

The creation of the constitution was a message to students that teachers honored their input and leadership. We teachers saw ourselves as authoritative, not authoritarian.. and students were in school to learn many things. But running a school was not at the top of the list. In setting up our school, constituting it if you will, we saw the creation of the school constitution as a powerful way to build the culture of community.

Both students and teachers take ownership and responsibility. It becomes a way to re-create the traditional roles of teacher and student. This is not a place where students have to react to traditional roles. As the Congress and school matured, it became obvious that if a student or teacher wanted to change something, it is up to the Congress to make it happen. What a powerful lesson in citizenship, in civics, in civility. As a civics teacher trained as a lawyer, I observed that community building and understanding were a result of this project. The students learned to negotiate, debate, listen, reformulate, compromise, vote, and then move on to the next aspect of formulating the document. The process also included learning much about articulating ideas; students learned the whole purpose of words and logical reasoning and how words and arguments can be misconstrued or misinterpreted from the original intent.

We find it interesting and not surprising that the whole constitution project mirrors the surrounding society. Both students and teachers expect more of the Congress - resolving issues and solving more problems. Congress sometimes proclaims an action but does not follow through; it promises to tackle an issue but fails to do so in a timely fashion or with appropriate resolve. Similar to our own government, there is lots of talk; laws are passed that are either unfunded mandates or empty promises. There is some apathy or indifference, and only a small portion of students are actually involved in congressional issues. But if the issue has a relevant significance, such as the question of a dress code or the question of whether we say the pledge of allegiance or whether we have a prom, a greater number participate. On

the other hand, so many Congress participants are involved in active citizenship through service learning. For example, many students volunteered for the Wellstone campaign, whose headquarters was a mile from the school.

In congressional meetings, we often joke that we Americans complain and believe that being vocal is enough, in fact consider it a form of active citizenship. But if you want to change something at Avalon, you go through the Congress. We did in fact amend the original constitution.

Originally we had a judiciary. We also established peer mediation and the restorative justice circle. Some faculty had experience in restorative justice and alternative dispute resolution. So litigation was not the choice. We did not believe in winner versus loser.

The original judges were, except for one female student, white males who were bored and without purpose. They complained and kept conjuring up plans to "take over." For example, the judges considered investigating the "probable" misuse of computers by other students, as the advisers had too many other things to do. It was difficult for them initially to understand that they could not usurp the teachers' legal responsibilities and that possible suspensions involved privacy rights.

This is a holistic community; it is a non-punitive, win-win democracy at work in all its glory and imperfections. Students learn to be active citizens by living it out. Choosing not to participate and vote in fact becomes a right; but it is our hope that having a working constitution and a Congress will actually increase student and teacher understanding that active citizenship is a responsibility to self and to the commonwealth.

The Constitution of the School of Avalon

Preamble

We, the People of Avalon, in order to provide for a safe and productive learning environment, promote the obtaining and usage of knowledge for the benefit of those around us, and ensure general happiness, do ordain and establish this constitution for Avalon high school.

Article I: The Legislative Branch

Section I

All Legislative power herein shall be vested in a Congress of Avalon, which shall consist solely of that group of officials.

Section II
Congress: Organization and Powers of Impeachment

1. Congress is made up of any person choosing to take part.
2. Any person attending may vote, regardless of prior attendance. The only reason a person would not be a lowed to vote is if that person were removed from Congress.
3. For a person to be removed there must be a majority vote in favor of removing that person. Length of removal will be judged by remaining Congress members. If a person is removed three times, the person is no longer a lowed to take part in Congress.
4. No representative shall hold a position of higher power within the Congress, therefore, there shall be no Speaker of the House, nor any similar position.

Section III
Meetings of Congress

Meetings shall be held on a weekly basis, at whatever time is found convenient by the members of Congress (if there is free attendance we need a set time).

Section IV
Rules of Procedure

Minutes must be recorded at every meeting. The Person that records minutes at one meeting leads at the next.

Section V
Privileges and Limitations

1. Representatives of Congress shall be compensated with credit, and by no other means.
2. For a Congress member who has been removed three times to be reinstated, that member must first go through mediation, as well as be approved by Congress.

Section VI
Procedures for Passing Bills, Executive Veto

1. Congress is charged with passing Bills.
2. Any member of the school may propose a Bill to the Legislative body, whether they are a student or a staff member.

3. A Bill must pass through Congress with a majority, after which it must be passed through the Executive branch, also with a majority vote.
4. For a Bill to be vetoed there must be a majority vote within the Executive branch in favor of such a veto.
5. A Bill may not be re-proposed for one block.

Section VII
Powers Delegated to Congress

1. The Representatives of the student body shall report all meeting information to their peers.
2. Congress may make, modify, or disband any law applying to students or the student/advisor relationship so long as it is not unconstitutional or against any higher-level laws.
3. Congress reserves the right to declare emergency or follow up meetings that are not scheduled.
4. Congress may form committees to organize, control, and lead any and all social events, including but not limited to the All School Meetings, Presentation nights, Public Relations tours, School Dances, and other events called to order.

Section VIII
Powers Denied to Congress

1. Congress may not override decisions made by higher-level laws, including, but not limited to the School Board, School District, Minnesota Government, or US Federal Law.
2. Congress may not be involved in or perform any disciplinary actions, as those are reserved for the Mediators.
3. Congress may not override the Executive veto.
4. Congress may not place restrictions on other branches of Government.

Article II: The Judiciary Branch

Section 1
Division of Branch Tenure of Office

1. The Judiciary branch of Avalon should consist of the Mediation Council.. The Mediation Council will consist of Peer Mediators as well as the Circle Process Group.

2. Any student who attends the mediation training may be a Mediator.
3. Mediators will facilitate communication to resolve individual student/student or student/advisor issues.
4. There will be a minimum of three trained Peer Mediators.
5. The Circle Process Group will address school issues through a Talking Circle and bring resolutions to Congress.

Section II
Jurisdiction

1. The Judicial Branch will be committed to Restorative Justice
2. The Judicial Branch will handle all cases that are not in violation of higher laws.

Article III: Executive Branch

1. The Avalon staff shall form the Executive Branch
2. The Executive Branch shall be responsible for upholding all higher laws.
3. The Executive Branch is permitted to veto laws made by Congress.
4. It is the responsibility of the Executive Branch to enforce the laws.

Article IV: Governing Body

Avalon School guarantees all students a democratic single-party government, and will follow all procedures as such.

Article V: Amendment Procedures

Any member of the school may propose an amendment, or Bill, whether they are students or staff, to the Legislative Branch.

First Amendment
Bill of Rights and Responsibilities

1. Every person has the right to bring someone to mediation.
2. Every person has the responsibility to attend mediation when asked at a reasonable time.
3. Every person has the right to be treated with respect and dignity.

4. Every person has the responsibility to treat others with respect and dignity.
5. Every person has the right to her or his own personal space.
6. Every person has the responsibility to respect other people's personal space.
7. Every person has the right and responsibility to try.
8. Every person has the right to ask why.
9. Every person has the responsibility to question themselves and their actions in times of duress.
10. Every person has the right to speak and communicate her or his views as long as they are respectful to others.
11. Every person has the responsibility to listen at all times to whoever is speaking.
12. Every person has the right and responsibility to be involved and participate here at Avalon High School.

References

Boyer, E. (1995). The basic school. Princeton, NJ: Carnegie Foundation for the Advancement of Teaching.

Boyte, H. (1995). Reinventing citizenship - The practice of public work. St. Paul: University of Minnesota Extension

Chapter 7

Cultivating Life Skills at a Project-based Charter School

Scott Wurdinger & Walter Enloe examine the results of an alumni survey revealing how students reflect on what they learned at Avalon.

Surveys that focused on academic and life skill development were collected from alumni who attended Avalon Charter School in St Paul, Minnesota. Avalon is a small public charter school that uses project-based learning as their primary teaching method. Forty-two alumni responded to the online survey. Students ranked life skills such as creativity, problem solving, and time management extremely high, whereas academic skills such as note taking and test taking were ranked much lower. Students graduate from this school with a strong sense of purpose and self-confidence, which helps them become productive members of society.

Introduction

Avalon Charter School was organized as a 'liberal arts' school in St. Paul, Minnesota in 2001 by a founding group of civic activists, pragmatic visionaries and some likeminded parents. A dedicated staff was hired who wanted to create a small 'people centered' secondary school of outstanding character. The school would be characterized by a shared vision of student and teacher ownership and collaborative teaching and learning with parents as full partners. The school's stakeholders co-created a highly innovative curriculum based on project-based learning and small seminars. Locally and globally, the world would be the classroom.

The school was created as part of a $4 Billion Bill and Melinda Gates Foundation initiative to ensure all students graduate from high school ready for college. This school assumes that when students have a sense of ownership of their work and the life- world of their school, students' achievement will increase. The centerpiece of the school's curriculum and instruction focuses on project-based learning that is self-directed and initiated through the students' passions and interests.

Avalon is one of the flagship learning communities of the EdVisions-Gates Project, funded in part by the Bill and Melinda Gates Foundation to create small 'world-class' schools (see edvisions.coop website). To judge a school's effectiveness on the international stage or in a local community, we need more than accountability testing systems of literacy and reasoning. We also need to cultivate, support, and take into account the life-world of students, their attitudes toward living and learning, their behaviors, their character. 'What we need if we are to judge schools effectively is a means by which schools can be assessed as cultures that create sets of relationships, norms of behaviors, and values and obligations that lead to the development of healthy and productive adults (Newell and Van Ryzin, 2007: 465–466).

In 1994 EdVisions Cooperative was created for the purpose of 'creating a professional association of teacher/owners that contract with a school board to supply a learning program'. It is based upon true site-based management and dynamic and flexible decision-making (EdVisions, 2008, n.d.). In 2001 the Bill and Melinda Gates Foundation awarded a grant to EdVisions for the purpose of replicating the project-based learning model that was used at the first EdVisions school called Minnesota New Country School (MNCS). It was at this point that EdVisions Inc., a non-profit organization, was formed to oversee the replication process. Since 2001, EdVisions Inc. has created more than 45 schools across the US modeled after MNCS, including Avalon.

EdVisions schools' 'design essentials' are characterized by four main themes that are embodied in the Avalon Charter School:

1) a self-directed, project-based learning program; 2) a student-centered democratic culture; 3) the use of authentic

assessment; and 4) teacher ownership and accountability (p. 468). Project-based learning at Avalon requires continuous conversation, discussion, and evaluation between advisors and students. Students identify a project they would like to do, fill out a project proposal form, negotiate the details of the project with their advisors and advisory committee, do the project, and present it to their advisory committee as an exhibition. Much of the time students work alone on their own projects, primarily because of their own specific interests, however students are a lowed to collaborate when they have similar interests in a project. Projects are broad ranging and might include things like designing museums, developing software programs, creating videos and movies, and creating documentaries through pictures (Newell, 2003). Depending upon their complexity, these projects may take a few days or several months to complete. When students finish a project they demonstrate their level of understanding by doing an exhibition for their advisory group, who consist of peers, advisors, community members, and parents. After the exhibition, advisors and students sit down together and discuss what curriculum state standards have been met, and how many credits they will receive for their work. In their senior year, students complete a 300–350 hour 'Senior Project' with a public presentation of their study (Thomas et al., 2005).

Students must complete all of the state standards so they are provided a copy of the standards when they enroll and are asked to be mindful of how they might complete these standards through their projects. Students move through this process at their own pace and finish their high school education when they have met all the mandatory state standards. Advisors work closely with students to make sure that all standards have been addressed through their project work. Some students graduate earlier than their traditional counterparts and others graduate later.

Avalon's approach to learning is quite different than the lecture format used by many educators, because with PBL, students take control of their own learning by choosing projects that are relevant and meaningful to their own lives. The theoretical underpinnings of the project method rely heavily on Dewey's (1938) 'pattern of inquiry'. The pattern of inquiry consists of six steps, however Dewey explains that his theory is similar to the scientific method and highlights four basic steps. He explains that a relevant problem (step one) causes perplexity and desire to find an answer, which is then followed by creating a plan (step two), testing the plan against reality (step three), and reflecting on its worth (step four). The planning and testing phases of this learning process are critical to project-based learning. Designing and building projects require students to solve problems and test out their ideas to determine solutions. Responding to instructor questions and reciting back information, which is a common teaching method in traditional education, a low students to talk, but learning becomes inspirational and exciting when students create plans to build projects and test them against reality.

Creating a web site, building a learning portfolio, performing an experiment, creating a piece of artwork, or building something off a blueprint, all require students to plan and test ideas in order to determine their worth. For Dewey learning meant doing something with the subject matter aside from reciting and memorizing information. Like Dewey, Avalon's philosophy is based on students' interests and a lows them to choose relevant meaningful projects that they create, design, and build (Thomas et al., 2005). Students at this school are given the freedom to determine their own projects and work at their own pace, and the advisors act as guides or facilitators of the learning process.

Since this approach is highly student centered and a lows students freedom to work at their own pace, it provides opportunities to practice life skills such as time management, problem solving, and responsibility. This approach to learning has the potential to teach not only academic content, but also life skills that are critical in helping young adults to become productive members of society.

Methods

Alumni from Avalon Charter School were surveyed in this study. The surveys were collected through Survey Monkey and analyzed by the three researchers. Avalon School has 154 graduates from 2003 to 2009. The school had email addresses for 120 of these graduates. Kevin Ward, the Avalon Advisor in charge of Alumni Relations, believed that only 100 of these addresses were viable at the time when he sent out the letter explaining the research and the survey links. Survey Monkey was open for two weeks and 42 responses were collected.

The survey questions focused on the educational experiences students had at this charter school. Questions centered on things such as life skills, academic skills, advantages of attending this school, and success.

There was no control group used in this study primarily because the surveys were designed specifically for schools using project-based learning. This survey would be difficult to administer to a large traditional mainstream US high school. The survey was designed as an online survey using Survey Monkey, and web links were sent to the alumni to complete the survey. The researchers created letters of explanation and consent forms, which were sent to all participants. The alumni list consisted of students that attended the school over the past seven years. Some of these alumni attended college and others did not. The surveys were posted online for 10 weeks in order to provide ample time for participants to fill them out and submit them.

The survey asked participants to rank their competency levels on different types of skills using a 1–5 Likert scale based on the following ratings: 1= poor, 2 = fair, 3 = satisfactory, 4 = good and 5 = excellent. Skills were categorized under two headings: Academic Skills and Life Skills.

Academic skills	**Life skills**
Writing	Creativity
Math	Problem solving
Verbal	Decision-making
Listening	Time management
Study skills	Finding information
Note-taking skills	Learn how to learn
Test-taking skills	Responsibility
	Team player

The skills identified under Life Skills were originally identified by the Secretary's Commission on Achieving Necessary Skills report as important life skills needed to be productive members of a work community (2001).

The yes/no questions asked survey participants if they felt the charter school experience had given them advantages over their peers in different settings. The alumni survey also asked if the Avalon Charter School experience provided them with advantages over their college classmates and co-workers.

Finally, the survey asked several open-ended questions. One question asked participants to identify the three most important things they learned at Avalon, and another asked participants to define success. An example of the alumni survey can found in the Appendix. There were a total of 42 alumni surveys collected, however not all 42 responded to each question.

Results

Forty-two alumni responded to the online questionnaire (these alumni graduated from high school between 2004 and 2009). The first question on the alumni survey asked respondents about their post-secondary accomplishments. Ten responded to the question of attending technical programs: two completed a program, seven are currently enrolled and one dropped out. Of the 40 alumni who made written responses, three (8%) completed their undergraduate education; 24 (57%) are currently enrolled and seven (16.7%) began but did not finish college. On the master's level education three students began academic programs but only one earned a masters degree. The final question in this section asked whether students were currently employed. Of the 40 who responded 27 (67.5%) are currently employed and 13 (32.5%) are unemployed.

The second section asked the alumni if they chose to attend Avalon school (88%) or if their parents chose the school (12%). They were then asked to rank (1 = poor, 5 = excellent) their overall academic performance before attending Avalon. The average rating before attending Avalon was 3.45, and their performance at Avalon was 4.41. Their overall academic performance after graduating from high school if applicable was 4.35.

The next section asked respondents to rank a list of academic and life skills using the same Likert scale (1= poor, 2 = fair, 3=satisfactory, 4 = good, 5 = excellent). The following table shows the percentage of students who ranked the skill as either good or excellent.

Academic Skills	
Writing	93
Math	48
Verbal	88
Listening	88
Study skills	82
Note-taking skills	54
Test-taking skills	47

Life skills	
Creativity	93
Problem solving	88
Decision-making	86
Time management	84
Finding information	95
Learn how to learn	91
Responsibility	91
Team player	73

The last section was composed of six open-ended questions providing for a written response. The first question asked students to identify the three most important things they learned at Avalon School. The answers varied and were coded according to themes mentioned most often by respondents.

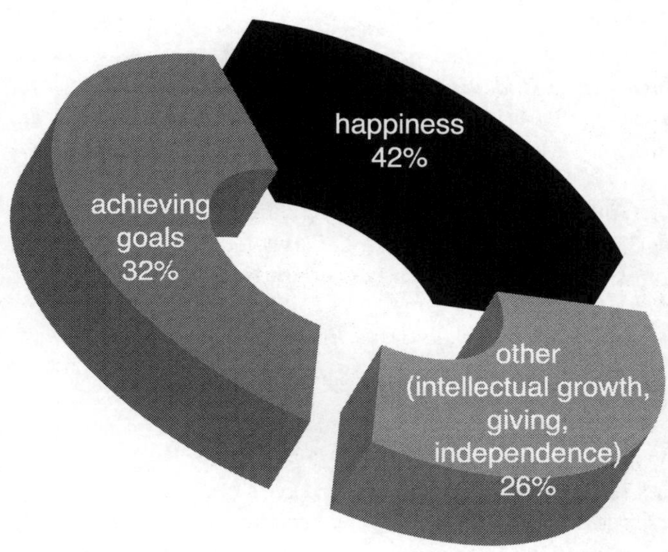

The next question asked alumni to reflect on whether there were broader life skills and/or knowledge they needed to reach their future goals that they did not receive at Avalon High School. All 42 alumni answered the question. Sixty-seven percent (33) responded no; 33 percent (nine) responded yes. Fifteen respondents made written comments, which fell into several categories: four respondents suggested the need for a stronger curriculum in math, science or test taking (one commented, 'Test skills but I believe Avalon turns out a well-rounded adult'); five alumni wrote of skills learned ('engaging community', 'life lessons') and 'the independence and confidence I needed'. Another person noted that he/she 'was not prepared for most stuff in college'; two were incomplete responses and one noted, 'No school can teach everything. It is not failing!'

When asked if Avalon gave them advantages over their college classmates, 41 of the 42 answered the question: 88% (36) said yes, 12% (5) said no. Written responses from this question fell into four categories: time management (11), academic skills (11), lifeskills (nine) and other (five). Alumni comments included the following:

I was way better at time management; writing papers longer than five pages scared lots of freshmen; had self- editing skills; I was more comfortable with freedom; then the intangibles – so many kids had come from different environments to a liberal arts high school – crucial point, I came from Avalon.

A strong advantage for me – managing study time between classes. Most students were used to sitting in classes all day and having to make time to study; it was easier for me to incorporate study into my everyday schedule.

Time management, and personal maturity (I had three years of independence at Avalon, my college classmates had none), independent studies, networking skills.

I knew what a syllabus was, how class structure and meeting only several times a week – no problems writing papers and doing research.

I was better prepared in reading, writing, being organized and responsible to get my assignments in on time. Project based learning helped my focus in college as well as my ability to communicate with others. Avalon gave me excellent writing, listening, reading comprehension and time management skills.

[Avalon had] a semi-structured system rather than just assignments to be done; it gave me an edge in creative thinking. Avalon overall very similar to college which is not what I hear from other students.

Avalon increased my ability to pursue things I want to learn (unlike many students) plus advantages in making strong, well thought out presentations.

Nine of the 33 written responses focused on life-skills. 'I'm a killer at studying and actually have a life-plan.' One wrote that an advantage he had over other students is 'working on my own – not to rely on the instructor (e.g. if I have a question, I can figure it out on my own . . . I know how to learn without being handed specific guidelines' and another alumnus indicated that 'I was able to critique my own work and self-manage my performance much better than others.'

In response to the question did Avalon School 'prepare you to reach your goals after graduation', 41 answered the question and one skipped. Some 90.5 percent responded yes while 9.5 percent responded no. Of 27 written comments the following categories are noted for college (seven), goal setting (five), independence, professional networking, life-skills (12), not prepared, not sure (four). Alumni comments included the following:

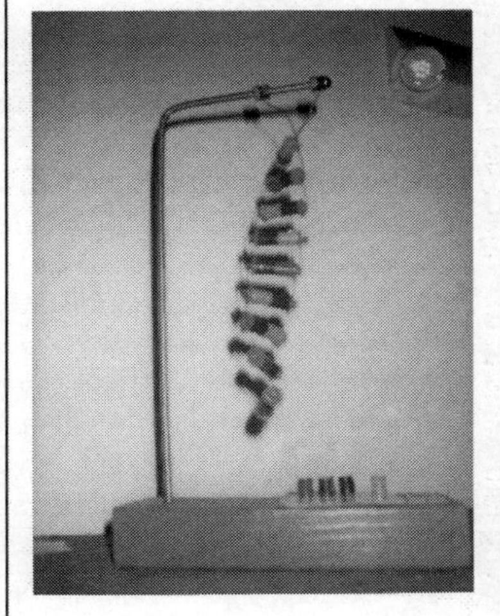

Because of all the hurdles I overcame and goals I did reach, I now know I can do things that terrify me and maybe even excel at them.

Avalon helped prepare me to reach my goals after graduation by giving me constant support throughout my time in high school which instilled confidence in me that my goals were attainable.

[Avalon] taught me to reach my goals, hard work, creativity, risk-taking and never being afraid to ask for help. Avalon taught me to work on my own create what I want to do in life.

When asked if the Avalon School experience gave them 'any advantages over your peers in your career after graduation', 34 students responded to the question while eight skipped it. Of those responding, 79 percent (27) wrote yes while 21 percent (seven) wrote no. There were 27 written responses in the following categories: time management (six), community involvement (two) and interpersonal conflict resolution (two) were reported as was life-skills (10). Five responded they were still in college and two were not applicable. Comments included:

When I attended (college) I was baffled at how much help other students needed to plan their schedule. At Avalon it was assumed you would design your own four year plan, not rely on your educators.

Avalon got me interested in being a community member – reason I was so involved in so many activities in college not only made my resume look better, it's given me a lot of valuable experiences that I would not get otherwise.

I explain Avalon and ace almost any job interview.

Avalon taught me how to network, how to handle job interviews, and how to function in professional communities.

Better time management, experiences working with people of different ages/backgrounds and taking responsibility for self.

I can deal with workplace conflict better than anyone I know and I know how to work creatively in many situations.

When asked if alumni felt that the Avalon School experience gave them any 'advantages over your peers in life', 41 responded and one skipped. Some 88 percent (35) of alumni responded yes while 12 percent (six) responded no to the question. There were 27 written responses which fell into the following categories: more confident, accomplished, passionate (six), more flexible, adaptable (two), other life-skills (seven), value community (four), school, graduate planning (four); and four were not applicable.

Because of projects I did, especially my senior project, I feel I've already accomplished a huge task in my life. I know a lot of high school grads from other schools [who] do not have this kind of experience already behind them. And I believe it will serve as a source of inspiration for me – it will make me want to do even bigger and better things in my future.

A similar response remarked:

I feel Avalon gave me the ability to view the world in a lens that is not entirely black and white; I am continually very grateful for Avalon for giving me skills to live in community, to see the world holistically, to be friends with people not exactly like me, and to understand that grades and test scores are not the most important things in life.

Avalon gave me advantages in life by igniting my passion for learning so even when I'm not in school; I am continually searching for ways to better my life and keep myself an active member of community.

Avalon helped teach me the value of community; Avalon taught me to find my goals and dreams and run after them.

I see learning and school as an enjoyable challenge and am more motivated to continue school than some peers. Self-reliance and independence allow me to direct my life where I want to go with less outside support.

I understand and respect community; I know how to deal with people from all sorts of backgrounds.

When asked to define success, responses fell into five categories.

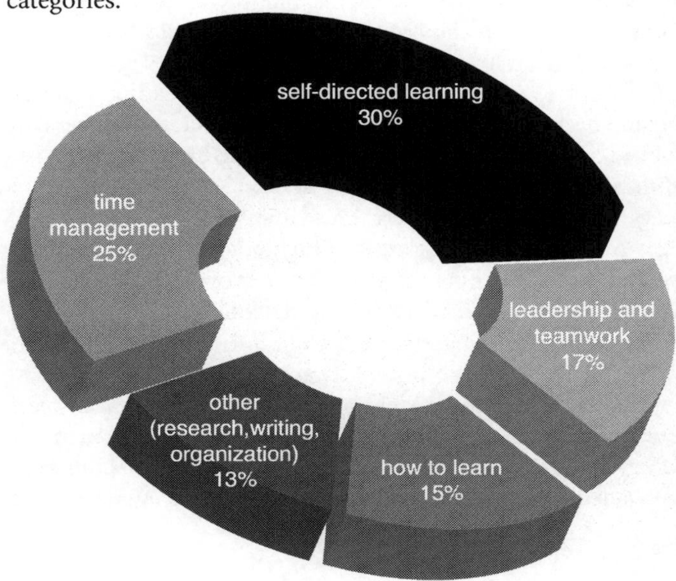

Discussion

In traditional school settings students learn how to take instructions from teachers, do their homework, memorize information for tests, and follow orders, but learning life skills appear to be lacking. Life skills such as creativity, time management, problem solving, and learning how to learn are usually not an intentional part of a high school curriculum, and therefore, students do not necessarily learn these skills until after they graduate. Students at Avalon Charter School however are doing exceptionally well in learning important life skills. Small advisories at this school, consisting of a teacher and 10–16 students, lends itself to a more personal education environment, but research indicates that project-based learning is a key factor in helping students learn important life skills.

In a study conducted at Minnesota New Country School, also an EdVisions project-based learning school, Wurdinger and Rudolph (2009) found that students ranked life skills extremely high. For instance, when combining the good and excellent rankings, creativity, finding information, problem solving, and learning how to learn were near or above 90 percent. The combined good and excellent rankings on the Avalon Alumni Survey were very similar. When combining good and excellent rankings all but one life ski l (being a team player) were ranked in the mid-80s to mid-90s. The Avalon alumni believe strongly that they learned valuable life skills while attending this school.

Academic skills however, were less impressive. When combining good and excellent rankings there were three skills that were in the 40th and 50th percentile: note-taking skills was 54 percent, test-taking skills was 47 percent and math skills was 48 percent. Students do not take tests at this school because they focus on projects, which is the reason why test-taking and note- taking skills were ranked low. Math is a difficult subject to teach using project-based learning which may be why this ranking was low.

So why are life skills ranked higher by alumni from these project-based learning schools? One reason might be because these schools are student centered. Students are given the freedom to design and create their own projects. Projects created by teachers do not generate the same level of interest and passion as those created by the students. When students create them they have relevancy and meaning. For example, when asked the question, 'Do you feel this charter school gives you advantages over your peers in more traditional public schools?' several students stated that they learn more because they get to do projects on whatever they are interested in. Often times these projects have practical ends such as making a lure to be used for fishing, or constructing a web site to start a small business. When students are responsible for designing and completing projects that have useful ends, they will use their creativity, and problem solving skills to carry out the necessary steps, possibly solving multiple problems along the way, in order to complete their projects. They invest time and effort in their work and take ownership of their projects.

Motivation may be another factor. In these environments students are not forced to learn by taking tests and having to memorize information. They are free to choose something from their own interest and are evaluated based on the quality of the project and their presentation of the project. Several students mentioned on the survey that they enjoy the freedom that Avalon provides because it has helped them become more self-directed and responsible for their actions.

In some cases students that have a sloppy project or poor presentation are required to do more research, fix their projects, and do their presentations again. The process continues until they reach a level of quality agreed upon by their advisory committee. For instance, an advisory committee may agree that a student has to streamline navigation procedures to make a web site design more user-friendly before granting credit for the project. Motivation is intrinsic because students desire to improve upon their projects, especially if they will be using them in real world settings.

Students learn that mistakes are valued and are part of the process. They learn that their advisory committee is a resource that can help them improve their projects, rather than authority figures that have the power to mark down their grade. Several students commented that they are treated more like equals at this school and teachers treat them with more respect. Learning to use their committee as a resource fosters self-confidence and leadership skills. Through this process students begin to realize that they are equals, and mistakes are seen as an important part of the learning process.

Time management is an ever-present part of the students' school day as well. Advisors check in on students and help guide the learning process but the student is responsible for staying focused and on track. The PBL process is structured requiring learning proposals, learning logs, daily check-ins, and eventually presentations. After doing a couple of projects, students realize that if they don't stay focused they will fall behind and may not graduate on time. Learning to manage time takes longer for some than others, but eventually most students realize how important this skill is if they want to do well and graduate on time.

Ultimately, this approach to learning is helping Avalon students learn how to be self-directed. Many students stated on the survey that this school has a lowed them the freedom to learn on their own and become more responsible for the completion of their own projects. Learning to be more independent was mentioned frequently and this can only be learned by providing students with freedom to do their own work and struggle through their own mistakes.

Conclusions

The data collected from this research study clearly indicate that students are learning important life skills, and that a project- based learning curriculum provides them with opportunities to learn and practice these skills. Obtaining and using these skills resonates throughout many of their answers on the survey and most alumni believe that this school provided them with advantages over classmates, peers, and co-workers. Equipping individuals with these skills carried over into post-secondary experiences and a lowed them to become more confident self-directed learners in higher education settings. Traditional public schools may want to take a closer look at this curriculum and implement some project-based learning in their own settings to help students acquire these important life skills.

Success for these students seems to go well beyond college completion and includes important values like happiness, reaching personal goals, and the betterment of others. Students have a mature view of reality and understand that success is not necessarily measured by degrees completed, but by being involved in experiences that promote personal growth and happiness. Students leave this school prepared for the challenges of life and are motivated to better themselves and the world around them.

Further research could look at the personalized learning that occurs at these small charter schools and how the teacher/student relationship might foster a more meaningful learning environment. In addition a deeper look at the project-based learning process is needed and how this process might be useful in more traditional public high schools.

The author can be contacted via email at:
scott.wurdinger@mnsu.edu

Appendix 1: Alumni survey

Education:

Please choose the option that best describes your educational attainment after high school AND your area of study.

Trade or Technical Certification
•Completed
•Currently enrolled
•Began, but did not finish
•Area of Study ~ Please Specify:

Undergraduate Education
•Completed
•Currently enrolled
•Began, but did not finish
•Area of study ~ please specify:

Master's Level Education
•Completed
•Currently enrolled
•Began, but did not finish
•Area of study ~ please specify:

Post Master's Degree Education
•Completed
•Currently enrolled
•Began, but did not finish
•Area of study ~ please specify:

Current Employment
•Unemployed
•Current Occupation:

What years did you attend this charter school?

Did you choose to attend this charter school?
•Yes, I chose to attend
•No, my parents chose for me
•Other, please specify

Please rank the following:

1 2 3 4 5
Poor Fair Satisfactory Good Excellent

My overall academic performance prior to attending this charter school
1 2 3 4 5

My overall academic performance at this charter school
1 2 3 4 5

My overall academic performance after graduating from high school (if applicable)
1 2 3 4 5

In what ways did your charter school experience prepare you for life after graduation?

Academic Skills

Writing Skills 1 2 3 4 5

Math Skills 1 2 3 4 5

Listening Skills 1 2 3 4 5

Study Skills 1 2 3 4 5

Note Taking Skills 1 2 3 4 5

Test Taking Skills 1 2 3 4 5

Life Skills

Creativity 1 2 3 4 5

Problem Solving 1 2 3 4 5

Decision Making 1 2 3 4 5

Time Management 1 2 3 4 5

Finding Information 1 2 3 4 5

Learned How to Learn 1 2 3 4 5

Responsibility 1 2 3 4 5

Being a Team Player 1 2 3 4 5

What were the three most important things you learned while attending this charter school?

Were there broader life skills and/or knowledge you needed to reach your future goals, but did not receive while attending this charter school? Yes No

Explain:

Do you feel that the charter school experience gave you any advantages over your college classmates? Yes No

Explain:

Do you feel that the charter school experience gave you any advantages over your peers in your career after graduation? Yes No

Explain:

Do you feel that the charter school experience gave you any advantages over your peers in life? Yes No

Explain:

Do you feel that this charter school prepared you to reach your goals after graduation? Yes No

Explain:

How do you define success?

Is there any additional information you feel is important to share?

References

Dewey J (1938) Experience and Education. Indianapolis, IN: Kappa Delta Pi. In How it all started. Retrieved 1st October, 2010, from http:/www.edvisions.com.

Newell R (2003) Passion for learning: how project-based learning meets the needs of the 21st century students. Lanham, MD: The Scarecrow Press, Inc.

Newell R and Van Ryzin M (2007) Growing hope as a determinant of school effectiveness. Phi Delta Kappan 88(6): 465–471.

Thomas D, Enloe W and Newell R (2005) The Coolest School in America. Lanham, MD: Rowman & Littlefield.

Wurdinger S and Rudolph J (2009) A different type of success: Teaching important life skills through project based learning. Improving Schools 12(2)

Chapter 8

The Damaging Effects of No Child Left Behind on the Learning Process and Schools that Have Risen Above it All

Scott Wurdinger - Minnesota State University-Mankato, USA Walter Enloe - Hamline University and EdVisions, USA

a sobering report published by the Center on Education Policy (2010) recently came out on the efficacy of No Child Left Behind (NCLB). The bottom line is, it does not work at a l! In Minnesota alone over half the schools in the state did not make Adequate Yearly Progress (AYP). Here are some key findings of this report:

- About one third of U.S. public schools did not make AYP based on tests administered in school year 2008-09. In nine states and the District of Columbia, at least half the public schools did not make AYP in 2008-09.
- In a majority of the states (34 including D.C.), at least one-fourth of the schools did not make AYP.
- The percentage of public schools not making AYP varied greatly by state, from 5% in Texas to 77% in Florida. These differences among states do not necessarily reflect the quality of schools; rather, they are likely due to state variations in standards, tests, cut scores for proficient performance on those tests, and methods for calculating AYP (2010, p.).

How did our education system end up in this situation and is there a viable alternative? In 2001 No Child Left Behind (NCLB) was passed by Congress and states began creating curriculum standards. After the standards were developed, standardized tests were created to assess students' knowledge of these standards. When student test scores became the mechanism to assess student learning, as well as to hold teachers accountable, teachers began teaching to the test. The most efficient way to teach to the test is by using the "lecture format" because it a lows teachers to dole out large amounts of information in short amounts of time. The problem however, is that this method kills motivation and inspiration to learn.

The content of the curriculum is obviously important in piquing student interest. In her book The Death and Life of the Great American School System (2010) Ravitch writes about the importance of first developing a strong curriculum, but a strong curriculum delivered poorly for the purpose of raising test scores will leave our students bored and disengaged.

Most educators can agree on the ends of education. Leave no child behind is an admirable goal, but what teaching method should educators use to get there? If a teacher relies solely on direct instruction, then the most important content may be nothing more than a meaningless string of words coming out of the teacher's mouth. If students are forced to be passive learners and sit and listen to teachers talk, then it doesn't matter what is said in the lecture, deep learning and the ability to apply information will not happen.

Research shows that a student's attention span is only 20 minutes (Hoover, 2006, p.469). Students lose interest beyond this time limit. In schools we observe firsthand the negative effects of lecturing-students nodding off, texting on their phones, and working on their laptops completely disengaged from the lecture.

What skills are students learning when they take these tests? Are they learning how to solve problems, be creative, and become self-directed learners? Oddly enough, many individuals in the field of education believe in the value of these life skills, yet educators are forced to use a teaching format, that results in a mind numbing process and leads to apathy and boredom!

Is the current education system in the U.S. based on a false assumption? What if intelligence was based on one's ability to apply information rather than one's ability to memorize it? What if the best way to measure a person's intelligence was not through standardized testing but through performance testing?

In the current education system intelligence is based on how well students perform on standardized multiple-choice tests. But, if one's ability to apply information is a better way to measure learning, then most of what educators, schools, and school districts are currently promoting results in ineffective learning.

Text books are written to cover the state's curriculum standards, teachers lecture and teach to the test, students memorize the information for the tests, and all of this centers on one goal: raising test scores. The data that is used to drive instructional practices in order to meet AYP focuses on the wrong goal.

When the goal is high test scores, students are forced to memorize information. Educators should be using assessment tools that measure important skills such as problem solving, creativity, and self-directed learning.

If the primary underlying assumption is wrong, then everything that emanates from that assumption may also be wrong. A huge bureaucracy based on high stakes tests has been created, which may be based on an incorrect assumption. Teachers and students are the pawns in the system and are being held accountable for an inadequate process of learning.

Teachers need to be treated as professionals. Currently, most everything teachers do in their classrooms is based on NCLB. They are trapped, and this legislation is not only stifling the creativity in students but it is stifling teacher creativity as well. They should be managing their own classrooms according to what they believe are in the best interests of their students.

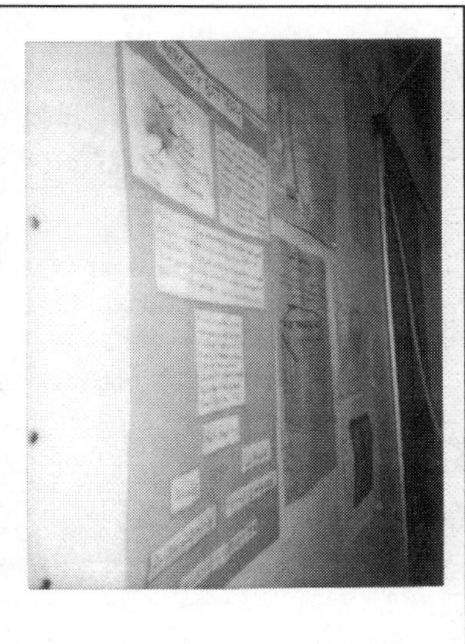

The most important experience that occurs in schools is what happens in the classroom between educators and students, and among students themselves. Educators should be challenging students to think, providing them with opportunities to be creative, letting them work in groups so they learn how to collaborate, and letting them learn by making mistakes. NCLB testing policies and procedures have created a death grip on teachers that prevents them from exercising their own judgment on how to best educate their students.

Teachers are forced to focus on increasing test scores. There are cases where not only students, but teachers are cheating (Amrein-Beardsley, Berliner, & Rideau, 2010). Teachers are resorting to cheating because their jobs are at stake.

Public education is producing students that simply cannot think for themselves. Students have learned how to retain large amounts of information, and many know how to do well on tests, but they don't know how to solve problems. When placed in situations where they are forced to solve a problem, many are paralyzed. How can students become self-directed learners if they are never given opportunities in school to make mistakes and figure things out on their own?

Learning is about using a complex process that involves multiple steps, and multiple trial and error episodes where students make mistakes and learn how to improve upon their solutions through these mistakes. According to Dewey, who wrote volumes on using direct experience for learning, the problem solving process entails identifying a problem, making a plan to solve it, testing the plan to see if it works, and reflecting on how to improve upon the solution (as cited in McDermott, 1973, pp. 101-119).

This process engages students in their learning because students are thinking, planning, and testing ideas, as opposed to just remembering facts. Thinking is a more complex process than remembering information, and it is an essential skill to survive and succeed in today's world. Life outside of school requires us to solve problems every day, yet today's students lack this skill.

Through his research Wagner identified a list of skills that employers believe are essential for students to have once they enter the work world. These skills are problem solving, collaboration, agility, initiative, oral and written communication, assessing information, and curiosity (2008, p,14-38). Employers are interested in hiring individuals who have the ability to ask probing questions, solve critical problems, can be productive team players, and are able to adapt to ever changing work environments.

The skills Wagner identifies are similar to the skills identified in the Secretary's Commission on Achieving Necessary Skills (SCANS) report titled What Work Requires of Schools that was published in 2000. This report found that skills such as creative thinking, decision making, problem solving, knowing how to learn, and reasoning were the skills employers valued the most, but were lacking in their young new hires (p. i).

The Partnership for 21st Century Skills is an organization that is also promoting the development of life skills students need to be successful once they leave school and enter the work world. Some of the skills they are promoting include: critical thinking and problem solving, communication, collaboration, and creativity and innovation (Partnership for 215t Century Skills website, n.d.).

Employers want to hire individuals that are curious about how the organization operates, and are able to speak and write effectively. The bottom line is, they want people who are self-directed and can figure things out on their own. These skills are essential to survival in today's work world, but Wagner found that they are sorely lacking in high school and college graduates.

Batista-Schlesinger argues the same point as Wagner. In her book, appropriately titled, The Death of Why she states, "America's employers aren't interested in test scores; they are interested in people who can think, question, adapt, and perform. We have created an educational environment devoid of curiosity, creativity and inquiry" (2009, p.6). She believes the education system is handing out answers to questions so that students can do well on tests, and this process is causing our students to no longer question anything. If they need answers they simply turn to the computer and find them on Google or other search engines.

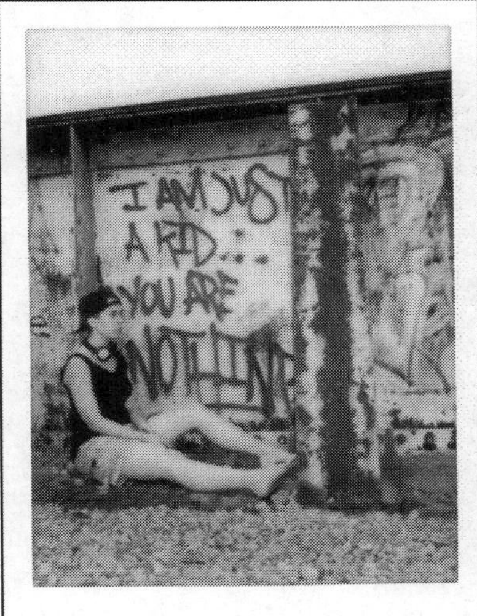

Students have been inculcated with a process of getting the answers they need and remembering them long enough to take the test. This problem is not going away and it is not the students' fault. Educators need to change their focus from answers to questions; from content to process. Educators should be free to use teaching approaches that will help students become problem solvers before they enter the work world.

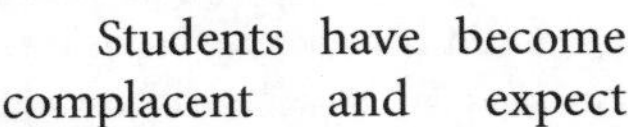

Students have become complacent and expect teachers and employers to give them the answers. They search, find, and plug in the answers. Their brains are not being used to create a plan and test it out to determine if the plan worked.

They have become entirely cerebral and lack the ability to solve real life problems.

In Newell and Van Ryzin's book Assessing What Really Matters in Schools (2009) they argue that schools are assessing the wrong thing. They argue that teachers should not be using test scores to assess how much information students can memorize, but rather, education should be assessing the student's level of hope for the future and motivation to learn. When students increase hope and motivation, they learn because they want to learn and are optimistic about their future.

Students ought to consider starting a peaceful intellectual revolution demanding more engaging teaching methods that a low them to be active participants in the learning process. They should be a lowed to regain their curiosity for learning and demand more freedom to explore ideas that are meaningful and relevant to their lives. Students should be provided with authentic learning and assessments, and have open honest discussions in their classrooms about how they learn best.

Allowing students to apply information turns them into researchers attempting to discover knowledge. This type of learning process takes on a whole different dimension. Students are typically motivated to learn using this process because they are attempting to find solutions to problems. With this process students are not memorizing information that has already been discovered, they are looking into the future and trying to discover their own answers to problems. One can look backwards in time at what has already been discovered, or one can be given a problem that leads out into the future and attempts to discover the unknown.

Certain project based learning schools are clearly helping students develop important life skills and -are pushing mainstream education to examine new teaching practices and techniques. EdVisions Inc. is an example of an organization that has helped create multiple project based schools based on innovative teaching practices using project based learning.

In 2001 the Bill and Melinda Gates Foundation awarded a grant to EdVisions for the purpose of replicating the project-based learning model that was used at the first EdVisions school called Minnesota New Country School (Jv1NCS). It was at this point that EdVisions Inc., a non-profit organization, was formed to oversee the replication process. Since 2001, EdVisions Inc. has helped create more than 45 schools across the United States modeled after MNCS (Doug Thomas, personal communication, October 5, 2011). EdVisions schools' 'design essentials' are characterized by four main themes:

- a self-directed, project-based learning program;
- a student-centered democratic culture;
- the use of authentic assessment; and
- teacher ownership and accountability (Newell & Van Ryzin, 2007, p. 468).

Project-based learning at these schools requires continuous conversation, discussion, and evaluation between advisors and students. Students identify a project they would like to do, fi l out a project proposal form, negotiate the details of the project with their advisors and advisory committee, do the project, and present it to their advisory committee as an exhibition. Much of the time students work alone on their own projects, primarily because of their own specific interests, however students are a lowed to collaborate when they have similar interests in a project.

Projects are broad ranging and some of the most recent ones include: working with a pastor setting up a business to raise funds for school supplies for inner city students, writing a weekly column in the local newspaper updating readers on activities and misperceptions about their school, and starting a saw mi l business and manufacturing a computer run saw. (Dee Thomas, personal communication, October 6, 2011). Depending upon their complexity, these projects may take a few days or several months to complete. When students finish a project they demonstrate their level of understanding by doing an exhibition for their advisory group, who consist of peers, advisors, community members, and parents. After the exhibition, advisors and students sit down together and discuss what curriculum state standards have been met, and how many credits they will receive for their work. (Newell, 2005, p. 34).

Students must complete all of the state standards so they are provided a copy of the standards when they enroll and are asked to be mindful of how they might complete these standards through their projects. Students move through this process at their own pace and finish their high school education When they have met all the mandatory state standards. Advisors work closely with students to make sure that all standards have been addressed through their project work. Some students graduate earlier than their traditional counterparts and others graduate later.

Research conducted at some of these schools clearly indicates that students who attend them have an advantage over their traditional counterparts when it comes to developing life skills. Alumni were surveyed at two of these schools (MNCS and Avalon Charter School) and asked to rank different academic and life skills they learned while attending these schools. Although standardized testing is not the driving force behind the project-based system, it is used for diagnostic purposes and for state accountability. Many educators doubt that students who have control over their own learning can achieve strong results in traditional methods of assessment. Not true; in the past nine years, average ACT and SAT scores at EdVisions schools have consistently surpassed national averages (Newell & Enloe,2008). At both schools students ranked the life skills extremely high. When combining good and excellent rankings, creativity, finding information, problem solving, and learning how to learn were near or above 90% at MNCS (Wurdinger & Rudolph, 2009, p. 122).

Something unique is going on at these schools, which should be embraced by traditional mainstream schools. Students at these schools actually enjoy going to school and are excited about their learning. Here are a few comments made by alumni from Avalon Charter School:

Avalon gave me advantages in life by igniting my passion for learning so even when I'm not in school, I am continually searching for ways to better my life and keep myself an active member of community.

Avalon helped teach me the value of community; Avalon taught me to find my goals and dreams and run after them.

I see learning and school as an enjoyable challenge and am more motivated to continue school than some of my peers.

Self-reliance and independence allow me to direct my life where I want to go with less outside support.

I understand and respect community; I know how to deal with people from all sorts of backgrounds (Wurdinger & Enloe, 2011, p. 91).

At the philosophical core of Ed Visions' schools is the teaching approach. Without this approach, learning would look very different. The teachers believe in this approach because they see students change over time and see that students are learning more than academic content; they are learning how to learn.

One of the key aspects to this approach is freedom. Teachers must provide students with freedom to make mistakes, otherwise it won't work. Freedom is critical in a lowing students to learn how to be responsible, how to organize their projects, how to take responsibility for their actions, and how to become self- directed learners.

Students leave these schools prepared for the challenges of life and are motivated to better themselves and the world around them. Teaching practices must change if the education system is to eliminate boredom and apathy in our high schools. It is time to move away from teaching to the test via the lecture format and start using teaching approaches that teach important life skills that will motivate students to learn and best prepare them to enter today's work world.

References

Amrein-Beardsley, A., Berliner, D.C. & Rideau, S. (2010) "Cheating in the first, second, and third degree: Educators' responses to high-stakes testing" Educational Policy Analysis Archives, 18(14). Retrieved October 30,2010 from http://epaa.asu.edulojs/article/viewI714.

Batista Schlesinger, A. (2009). The death of why: the decline of questioning and the future of democracy. San Francisco; CA: Berrett-Koehler Publishers, Inc.

Center on Education Policy. (2010). How many schools have not made adequate yearly progress under the No Child Left Behind Act. Retrieved on October 30,2010 from http://www.cepdc.org/index.cfm?fuseaction=document~ext.showDocumentByID&nodeID=1&DocumentID=303

Dewey, J. (1973).Pattern of inquiry. In 1.1. McDermott (Ed.). The philosophy of John Dewey (pp. 223-239). Chicago: University of Chicago Press. (Reprinted from Logic: The theory of inquiry, pp. 10i-119, by J.Dewey, 1938, Austin, TX: Holt, Rinehart, & Winston) .

Hoover, S. (2006). Popular culture in the classroom: Using video clips to enhance survey classes. History Teacher, 39(4), 467-478.

Huba, M. E.; & Freed, 1. E. (2000). Learner-centered assessment on college campuses: Shifting the focus from teaching to learning. Needham Heights, MA: A lyn & Bacon.

National Center for Public Policy and Higher Education (2006) Measuring Up 2006: The National Report Card on Higher Education, p. 7. Online: http://wwW.highereducation.org/reports/mup_ 06IMUP-06.pdf [accessed 12 May 2008].

Newell, R. (2005). The EdVisions project approach. In D. Thomas, W. Enloe & R. Newell (Eds.), The coolest school in America: how small learning communities are changing everything: (pp. 29-37). Lanham, MD: Scarecrow Education.

Newell R and Enloe W (2008) In Charge of Learning. Educational Leadership. 68(3).

Newell, R. & Van Ryzin M (2007) Growing hope as a determinant of school effectiveness. Phi Delta Kappan 88(6): 465-471.

Newell, R. & VanRyzin, M. (2009). Assessing what really matters in schools: creating hope for the future. Lanham, MD: Rowman and Littlefield Publishers.

Ravitch, D. (2010). The death and life of the great american school system: how testing and choice are undermining education. New York, NY: Basic Books.

Sax, L.J., Keup, 1. R., Gilmartin, S. K., Stolzenberg,E. B., & Harper, C. (2002). Findings from the 2000 administration of 'Your First College Year': National aggregates. Los' Angeles: University of California, Higher Education Research Institute.

SCANS Report: U.S. Department of Labor. What work requires of schools. Retrieved on 10105/2011 from:
http://wdr.doleta.gov/SCANS/

The Partnership for 21st Century Skills website. Retrieved June 26, 2011 from www.p2I.org.

Wagner, T. (2008). The global achievement gap: Why even our best schools don't teach the new survival skills our children need-and what we can do about it. New York, NY: Basic Books.

Wurdinger, S. D. & Enloe, W. (2011). Cultivating life skills at a project based charter school. Improving Schools. 14 (1)84-96.

Wurdinger, S.D. & Rudolp, 1. L. (2009). A different type of success: teaching important life skills through project based learning. Improving Schools. 12 (2), 117-131.

Chapter 9

Living Democracy Daily: Service-Learning and Active Citizenship

Walter Enloe, one of the founders of Avalon, describes Avalon as a student democracy.

We, the People of Avalon, in order to provide for a safe and productive learning environment, promote the obtaining and usage of knowledge for the benefit of those around us, and to ensure general happiness, do ordain and establish this constitution for Avalon High School.

-The 2001 Constitution of Avalon High School

A Case Study in Public Service

This chapter presents a case study of a school created in 2001 in St. Paul, Minnesota, as part of the $4 Billion Bill and Melinda Gates Foundation initiative to ensure that all students graduate from high school ready for college. Nationwide, just 70% of American students graduate from high school. Among African American, Hispanic, Native American, and low-income students, only 50% graduate. Avalon High School was created based on the assumption that when students have a sense of ownership of their work and the life-world of their school, and when academic service-learning is defined as servant leadership and active civic engagement, student achievement will increase.

Interdependent World

The changing world is increasingly complex and interdependent and is defined by ecological, technological, economic, political, and other frameworks. At the dawn of the 21st century, we face many daunting challenges, from global warming to social inequities, from tribal warfare to world conflict, from the threat of global ground zeroes like Hiroshima and the World Trade Center in New York. As Dr. Martin Luther King Jr. expressed in his last sermon days before his 1968 assassination: "The world is more and more of a neighborhood. But is it any more of a brotherhood? If we don't learn to love together as brothers and sisters, we shall perish together as fools (Washington, 1990, p. 245). In a world with increasing disparities between haves and have-nots, how can we prepare students to be responsible citizens locally and globally? How can we prepare them to lead, learn, and serve?

Recently, Minnesota's governor, following the lead of other states, initiated World-Class Students: From Nation Leading to World Competing (Minnesota Department of Education, 2008). Although Minnesota has a proud tradition of leading the nation in academic achievement, service-learning, and active citizenship, "our state and our students can no longer rely on our past success if we are to succeed in a more competitive global environment." The World-Class Students initiative "is designed to create a system of education for the 21st century, preparing Minnesota students to compete with students around the world." The World-Class Students initiative will help students to meet the demands of a more competitive global future by requiring every Minnesota high school to do the following:

1. High school must offer students at least one year of post-secondary education while in high school;
2. High schools must offer programs that support post-secondary access from the International Baccalaureate, AdvancePlacement, College in Schools, among others;
3. High schools must provide rigorous programs including career and technical courses in high demand fields and recognized by the business community;
4. Schools must forge community partnerships for meaningful work-based learning and internship.(MN Dept of Ed, 2008)

Although these "competitive" initiatives are a response to an increasingly global, international-minded world, we must also understand that the global future demands what is at the heart of active citizenship and service-learning: local and global cooperation, collaboration, mutual respect and understanding, and problem solving and reflection. One of the most powerful lessons I learned from 8 years as principal of the International School in Hiroshima is that, if you are not developing empathy, cooperation, and mutual respect among children sitting next to each other; or across town or in another state, you will have little success developing such values for "strange lands and friendly peoples" across the globe.

In the following case study, I describe how, at the beginning of the new millennium, a small group of St. Paul, Minnesota, parents and supporters purposefully constituted the Avalon High School. This process involved building, maintaining, and sustaining a civil learning community using leadership teams, study groups and advisories, a school, congress, restorative justice circles, peer mediation, and academic service-learning, all guided by a co-constructed school constitution and declaration of human rights and responsibilities. Avalon is one of the flagship learning communities of the EdVisions-Gates Project, funded in part by the Bill and Melinda Gates Foundation to create small "world-class" schools. (See the www.edvisions.com website for more information.)

EdVision Schools

To judge a school's effectiveness on the international stage or in a local community, we need more than accountability in testing systems of literacy and reasoning. We also need to cultivate, support, and take into account the life-world of students, their attitudes toward living and learning, their behaviors, and their characters. "What we need if we are to judge schools effectively is a means by which schools can be assessed as cultures that create sets of relationships, norms of behaviors, and values and obligations that lead to the development of healthy and productive adults" (Newell & Van Ryzin, 2007, pp. 465-466).

For the past 5 years, EdVisions has been actively researching its schools using a number of assessment tools and formative evaluations, including the Hope Study, which measures the growth in dispositions for success in life, in particular those values meeting the developmental needs of adolescents: autonomy, belongingness, and competence.

EdVisions's experience "reveals that when certain concepts are built into a learning community-concepts that value 'personhood' over ruthless efficiency and encourage student self-directedness and teacher/student ownership instead of top-down hierarchies - then that community can indeed foster healthy development" (p, 466). EdVisions schools' "design essentials" are characterized by four main themes: (a) a student-centered democratic culture; (b) a self-directed, project-based learning program; (c) the use of authentic assessment; and (d) teacher ownership and accountability (p. 468). These characteristics are embodied in Avalon High School, as described later (Newell & Van Ryzin, 2007).

In sum, much has to be done to overcome the present fixation on assessing school effectiveness solely using standardized tests and other traditional measures. The educators at Avalon believe, as does Comer of the Yale Child Study Center Project, that improvement in school culture must come first, "or the relationships needed to engage students in a powerful way won't be created" (Comer, 2005, p. 762). A founding group of civic activists, pragmatic visionaries, and like-minded parents organized Avalon High School as a liberal arts school. This group hired an outstanding, dedicated staff and strove to create a small, people-centered secondary school of exemplary character. The school is characterized by a shared vision of student and teacher ownership and collaborative teaching and learning, with parents as full partners. The school's stakeholders co-created a highly innovative curriculum based on project-based learning and small seminars. The world is the classroom. More specifically, some of the founders committed to supporting the United Nations declaration of 2001-2010 as the International Decade for a Culture of Peace and Nonviolence for the Children of the World by becoming a living, local symbol of mindfulness and peacefulness. The Quaker tradition of circles of trust, the Native American tradition of restorative justice, the Hamline University law school's international reputation for alternative dispute resolution, and the school's primary consultant influenced the school's mission and vision as a world-minded service-oriented community.

The evolving mission of the school is as follows: "The Avalon School is a strong, nurturing community that inspires active learning, local action, and global awareness." Its core values statement is:

Avalon expects and models respect for individuals, different cultures, the community, and the environment. The atmosphere is one of tolerance, integrity, equity, and safety. Avalon believes it is the responsibility of individuals to be engaged, active participants in their local and global communities. Visitors to Avalon will immediately recognize the sense of purpose, quality, and commitment that energizes this community.

Following the Minnesota New Country School model, Avalon High School will become a teacher-owned school and a member of the EdVisions Teacher Cooperative, established in 1994. As of 2008, Avalon High School has reconstituted itself as a Teacher Professional Practice Organization (TPPO), an autonomous collaborative, and remains a strong affiliate of both the EdVisions Cooperative and the EdVisions regional Center for the Coalition of Essential Schools. In its original documents, Avalon's founders stated that they would "build a school culture and a set of values centered on excellence and active citizenship" with a "global perspective" and that its constituents would "develop leadership opportunities for all participants. All members of the school community will be involved in decision making, and students will be given a real voice and stake in the school."

A few years earlier, several parent/founders (including the author of this chapter) had created Twin Cities Academy middle school in St. Paul (which the current and past mayors' children attended) as a school community emphasizing active citizenship. It became a learning place for building character and practicing active community involvement through enacting five core interrelated leadership and service values: active citizenship, respect, initiative, scholarship, and perseverance. We sought to integrate these leadership principles into the core mission and values of Avalon.

Active Citizenship

The creators of Avalon were also guided by the work of Harry Boyte and his partners (including teacher and civil rights activist Dorothy Cotton) at the University of Minnesota's Center for Democracy and Citizenship (CDC) and the leadership of Jim Keilsmeier at the National Youth Leadership Council (NYLC). I have deep-felt gratitude for apprenticing with democratic youth leaders as a partner and collaborator during the past 20 years. The active citizen and academic service-learning promoted by CDC and NYLC are often complementary. CDC's active citizenship executes everyday public work, including public problem solving by ordinary citizens in which governing is conceived for, by, and of the citizens (see the website www.publicworkorg). NYLC's academic service-learning, for example, is defined as follows: "Picking up trash on a riverbank is a service. Studying water samples under a microscope is learning. When science students collect and analyze water samples, document their results, and present their findings to a local pollution control agency that is service learning' (National Youth Leadership Council website). Active citizenship and academic service-learning emphasize learning through experience and not simply learning about phenomena. Both are based on interconnecting students and the community by identifying specific learning goals and developing projects that meet them, or by identifying a project and then exploring the many ways it can be tied to learning objectives or curricula.

In consideration of active citizenship and academic service-learning, Avalon's founders emphasize the development of democratic character as an essential component of a democratic school learning community. Although this school emphasizes rigorous academics and best practices, it is grounded in core ethical, democratic virtues: honesty, respect, compassion, self- discipline, perseverance, and giving that is learned through and not about. School members live out these core virtues with purpose by word and by deed. Boyer (1995) captures the living (ecocultural, organic, systemic) nature of such a school learning community:

But community just doesn't happen, even in a small school. To become a true community the institution must be organized around people .... What we are really talking about is the culture of the school, the vision that is shared, the ways people relate to one another .... Simply stated, the school becomes a community of learning when it is a purposeful place, a communicative place, a just place, a disciplined place, a caring place, and a celebrative place. (p. 18)

Democratic Service as Public Work

The teachers think that modeling democratic values daily is the best way to promote and perpetuate them so that they become integral to school culture. Democracy has value only when we recognize the humanity of each human being and her or his innate desire to be free and autonomous. Embodying the democratic virtues of civility and negotiation, collaboration and compromise, tolerance and mutual respect,

Avalon develops active citizens through active learning and engagement. The teachers create learning and leadership conditions through school meetings, advisories, committees, projects, and seminars so that students can constitute themselves as a self-governing community.

In the first year of Avalon, students in a two-block civics seminar, advised by teacher Carrie Bakken, created the constitution of Avalon High School. The Avalon constitution is based in part upon a class constitution that was established in Bernie and Martha Schein's class at the Paideia School in Atlanta and that has evolved over several decades. In the initial stages, the students experienced many struggles reminiscent of the challenges faced by the creators of the United States Constitution and by many other young democratic institutions. Students argued about whether they should have a constitution, much less a congress or student government, and many meetings were spent "discussing" the central issue of adult authority and teacher power. After the civics seminar, students wrote the initial version of the constitution, which then underwent many drafts. Subsequently, the whole school voted to accept it. Since that time, the document has gone through several more revisions; today the constitution governs the school and defines how the students and staff work together. It te ls members what their rights and responsibilities are as citizens of Avalon.

Avalon's constitution defines four branches of government: (a) the people individually and as a whole; (b) the legislative branch (student congress); (c) the judiciary (the Mediation Council consisting of peer mediators and the circle process group); and (d) the executive branch (the Avalon staff). Together they govern the school.

Another feature of the school's government that survived a rocky beginning before being amended to its present form is the judiciary branch. Initially, a group of dedicated students were appointed as judges in the judicial system. They waited patiently for court cases to be brought before them, planning to "sentence" each guilty offender with an appropriate punishment. But cases never materialized. One student discovered that the rest of the judges were beginning to conspire to fabricate cases, and the student brought this concern to the congress. The school realized that the traditional judicial process was not the way to address problems and offenses in this community. They changed the constitution to incorporate peer mediation and circle processes into the judiciary branch, which today is known as the Mediation Council. Peer mediators are students who are trained in mediation and who mediate issues that arise in the community between students or between students and staff. The circle process, based upon restorative justice philosophy, is another approach available to students and staff to identify issues and resolve conflicts. The school believed that congress and the circle process were such important parts of the community that they built meeting times into the weekly schedule for these groups. If students have issues they want to raise, they can present the issue to the circle for discussion. If the issue can be resolved in the circle, there is no further discussion. Sometimes circle issues are brought to congress and a Bill may be created. In addition, individual students may bring issues and Bills to congress.

When a Bill is submitted to congress, the participants vote on it. In the past few years, students have submitted numerous Bills to congress, and most have passed with some modifications. They include (a) a Bill requiring Avalon to offer sex education seminars twice a year; (b) a Bill a lowing students to read outside their advisories' areas (during an a l-school 30-minute reading period each day after lunch); (c) a Bill to establish a school-wide mandatory advisory cleaning period 15 minutes before the end of the school day.

When a Bill passes congress it is then submitted to the executive branch for approval. The executive branch can approve the Bill, approve the Bill with modifications, or reject the Bill; the executive branch can also invite parents to discuss the Bill or bring it to the school board before granting approval. If there are modifications to the Bill, the Bill then goes back to congress for approval. Once the Bill is approved, it becomes law. This system of governance has a lowed Avalon to build a strong community and face challenges with a team community approach. Students and staff know that when they have problems, they can discuss them with their advisor or any staff member, bring the issue to congress or circle, or ask for peer mediation. Students rely on one another to solve problems through myriad means, thereby helping each other deal with personal and social issues authentically, humanely, and often efficiently.

Two Concepts of Citizenship Service

Shigeo Kodama, a professor of educational thought at Ochanomizu University in Tokyo, has studied Avalon's governance process. In his study, "Two Concepts of Citizenship" (Kodama, 2003), he distinguishes between citizenship as volunteer service and citizenship as political action:

In volunteer activities [sic] young people do not have much time to think about the political meaning of their activity, and they are not given enough skill and competence of political action and judgment which are the indispensable factor of citizenship. Community service and volunteer activity will depoliticize the young people and prevent them from being active citizens.

He then describes how the advisors are teachers of academic subjects and facilitators of authentic community governance and leadership, encouraging students "to be active citizens in the public sphere." He contends that Avalon has two unique features. One is its institutional governance system, the EdVisions Cooperative, "a kind of governance system which is managed by the teachers themselves." The second is the Avalon constitution, which is the students' self-governance system and which is striking for its modeling of power relationships.

According to the Constitution students in Avalon compose (the) Avalon Congress and make their decisions). Teachers compose an executive branch and have a veto power to the students' decision(s). So in this system students not only have their own decision-making but also the power relationship between students and teachers could be visible. In this power relationship students could be trained as ... active citizens. (Kodama, 2003, p. 38)

Professor Kodama notes that Avalon's approach to democratic governance derives from the work of Harry Boyte and his partners. In Reinventing Citizenship (Boyte & partners, 1995), Boyte argues that, unlike traditional civics education, where one learns passively without civility about democracy and its institutions and processes, Avalon's approach is for students and adults to learn through democratic practices by living democracy daily in ordinary affairs and everyday practices.

Active, public citizenship begins and is grounded in our everyday institutional environments - the places wellive and work, go to school, volunteer, participate in communities of faith. It is public-spirited and practical: not utopian or immaculate but part of the messy, difficult give-and-take process of problem solving. Citizenship links our daily life and interests to larger public values and arenas. Through citizenship we build and exercise our power" (Boyte & partners, 1995, p. 16).

Conclusion

Avalon strives to embody a community where government is not simply for the people (which is the current American representational, professional politics, in which the generic citizen is an informed voter), but rather of the people and by the people, a form of active citizenship. This living democracy is a human ideal with all the constraints and opportunities inherent in the human condition. The founding of Avalon School was based in large part on Jean Piaget's theory of human development: his constructivist theory of learning, his activity pedagogy, his deep conviction that education should foster human rights and responsibilities (Article 26 Universal Declaration of Human Rights), and his commitment to student self-government (Piaget, 1948).

We believe very strongly that the basis for an authentic learning community is a school or learning organization in which the teachers are leaders and have ownership of their work lives, and lead, learn, and advise/teach together. We believe very strongly in a learning community where students are active learners and active citizens and are rightfully responsible for their actions of learning and leading. From EdVisions's reform efforts, we have learned that placing rigid curriculum, instruction, testing, and delivery systems in an environment that fails to meet adolescents' needs will not lead to long-term positive effects for students. The EdVisions experience leads us to believe that the new 3 Rs (relationships, relevance, and rigor) are more important than the old 3 Rs (reading, writing, and arithmetic). At EdVisions schools, "creating environments that a low for good relationships, relevant learning experiences, and rigorous assessment has created passionate, self- motivated, life-long learners" (Newell & Van Ryzin, 2007, p. 471). Avalon, a school in St. Paul, is such a citizen leader and service learning community.

References

Boyer, E. (1995). The basic school. San Francisco: Jossey-Bass.

Boyte, H. (2005)_ Everyday politics: Reconnecting citizens and public life. Philadelphia: University of Pennsylvania Press.

Boyte, H., & partners. (1995). Reinventing citizenship: The practice of public work. St. Paul: University of Minnesota Extension Service, www.extension.urnn.edu/distribution! citizenship/DH6586.html

Cairn, R, & Kielsmeier, J. (1995). Growing hope. St. Paul: N.Y.L.C.

Collay, M., Dunlap, D., Enloe, W., & Gagnon, G. (1998). Learning circles: Creating conditions for professional development. Thousand Oaks, CA: Corwin Press.

Comer, J. (2005, June). Child and adolescent development: The critical missing focus in school reform. Phi Delta Kappan, 28,
28-34.

Dirkswager, E. (Ed). (2002). Teachers as owners. Lanham, MD: Rowman & Littlefield. Education Evolving. (2005). Listening to student voices. Retrieved April 30, Z009, from http://www.educationevolving.org!studentvoices

Enloe, W. (1992) Education 2000: Rural Minnesota in the world (Vol. I). Washington, DC: ERIC/CRESS Clearing House on Rural Education, and Small Schools, U.S. Department of Education.

Enloe, W. (2002). Lessons from ground zero. St. Paul, MN: HU Press.

Friedman, T. L. (2005). The world is flat: A brief history of the twenty-first century. New York.

Farrar, Straus, Giroux. Greenleaf, R (2003), The servant leader within; A transformative path. Mahwah, NJ: Paulist Press.

Kodama, S, (2003). Two concepts of citizenship. Guidance and Education in High School No,156,2003.3, Tokyo (original in Japanese, English summary used in this paper).

Kolderie, T. (1988). What makes an organization want to improve? Ideas for the re-structuring ofpublic education. University of Minnesota, Hubert H. Humphrey Institute of Public Affairs. Minneapolis, MN.

Martin, A., Bakken, C., Rude, C., & Enloe, W. (2005). Creating a democratic learning community: The Avalon experience. In The coolest school in America (pp. 121-132). Lanham, MD: Rowman & Littlefield.

Minnesota Department of Education. (2008). World class students. St. Paul, MN.

Nathan, J. (1996). Charter schools: Creating hope and opportunity for American education. San Francisco.

Jessey-Bass. Newell, R, & Thomas, D. (2005). Less, more, and better: A five year evaluation report from EdVisions schools. Henderson, MN: EdVisions.

Newell, R, & Van Ryzin, M. (2005). Rigor, relevance, and relationships in educational reform: The story of the Hope Study. Retrieved April 30, 2008, from www.edvisions.edu.

Newell, R., & Van Ryzin, M. (2007). Growing hope as a determinant of school effectiveness. Phi Delta Kappan, 88(6),465-
471.

Newell, R, & Van Ryzin, M. (2008). Assessing what really matters in school.' Creating hope for the future. Lanham, MD: Rowman & Littlefield.

Piaget, J. (1948). The right to education in the modern world. In J. Piaget (1973), To understand is to invent, Chapter 2. New York: Grossman.

Piaget, J. (1969). The moral judgment of the child. New York: Free Press. (Original work published 1936)

Thomas, D., Enloe, W., & Newell, R. (2005). The coolest school in America. Lanham, MD: Rowman & Littlefield.

Washington, J. (1990). A testament of hope. New York: HarperOne.

Chapter 10

Two Concepts of Citizenship

Shigeo Kodama - from Guidance and Education in High School, No.156.,2003.3., Aoki publishers, Tokyo, original in Japanese. English Summary

In the national election of 2002 Republican party won both in Minnesota and the whole USA. But it is not relevant to say that this result represents the win of conservatism. As Lisa Disch, a political theorist of University of Minnesota says, Minnesotans voted for the third party candidates more than before. The traditional opposition between Republican and Democrats has begun to break down. It is at this point that Charter School movement gets a kind of significance in the political context in USA. Oscar Schefers, a manager of City Academy Charter School in St. Paul says that Charter School movement is a kind of hybrid of the Republican's emphasis on local control and the Democrats' emphasis on public finance for public school.

Judy Farmer, a member of Minneapolis Public School Board says that the political context of Charter School reform in Minnesota had been made during the period of governor Rudy Perpich. According to Farmer, the specific difficulty of sponsoring Charter School lies in evaluating the educational accountability.

What kind of citizenship public school should educate becomes the crucial matter in this context.

From volunteer to the public

Harry Boyte puts forward the importance of the political citizenship as is distinguished from the citizenship as volunteer. Harry Boyte is a Co-Director of the Center for Democracy and Citizenship of Humphrey Institute of Public Affairs in University of Minnesota. He is also a co league of Joe Nathan, author of Charter Schools, Jossey-Bass,1996.

In volunteer activity young people do not have much time to think the political meaning of their activity, and they are not given enough skill and competence of political action and political judgment which are the indispensable factor of citizenship. Community service and volunteer activity will depoliticize the young people and prevent them from being active citizens.

It is at this point that Harry Boyte's focusing on the political citizenship has a significant importance for the public education reform not only in US but also in Japan.

Teacher as political leader

Then how can we educate students for the political citizenship? Harry Boyte and his associates are now trying to introduce a Public Achievement teaching program into public education system. In this program the role of teacher in public school is very important. In this situation teachers are not only a instructor of academic subjects but also a kind of political leader who educate and train students to be a active citizens in public sphere. In order to make teachers political leader, teachers in public school should be given a freedom and self-governance of their own school. And I think Charter School could be a useful tool for creating such a situation.

For example I want to focus on Avalon Charter School in St. Paul. Walter Enloe in Hamline University , who is also a co- researcher of Harry Boyte, committed the foundation of this school. Avalon Charter school has two unique features. One is its governance system so called Edvision cooperative, a kind of self-governance system which is managed by teachers themselves.

The other feature is so called Avalon Constitution which ruled the students' self-governance system. According to the Constitution students in Avalon school compose Avalon Congress and make their own decision. Teachers compose an executive branch and have a veto power to the students' decision. So in this system students not only have their own decision making but also the power relationship between students and teachers could be visible. In this power relationship students could be trained as active citizens.

Shigeo Kodama, Professor
Graduate School of Education, The University of Tokyo
7-3-1 Hongo, Bunkyo-ku, Tokyo 113-0033, Japan phone/fax 81-3-5841-3938 http://homepage2.nifty.com/eduscikodama/

Chapter 11

Can Teachers Run Their Own Schools? Tales from the Islands of Teacher Cooperatives

Charles Taylor Kerchner with the assistance of Laura Steen Mulfinger, Claremont Graduate University, October 2010

In Arthurian legend, Avalon is "The Fortunate Isle." For the faculty and many of the 187 students, the Avalon School in St. Paul, Minnesota is also wonderfully detached from the mainland of public education. From the old coffee factory in which it operates to the individual student work-spaces, it doesn't look much like school at all.

Minnesota Teacher-Run Schools: 2009-2010
Results on the Minnesota Comprehensive Assessment Test

School, Grades & Enrollment		Percent Meets or Exceeds Expectations				Percent
	Grade	Math	Reading	Science	Made AYP	FRL (SE)*
State	All	64.69	72.41	48.83	No	36 [13]
Avalon: 7 thru 12: 172	All	45.76	76.19	37.25	Yes	22 [19]
Edvisions Off Campus School: 7 thru 12: 73	All	10.71	53.12	25	No	38 [14]
El Colegio Charter School: 9 thru 12: 90	All	0	9.09	**	No	89 [16]
Green Isle Community School: K thru 6: 90	All	51.16	62.79	**	Yes	32 [14]
Lafayette Public Charter School: K thru 8: 67	All	50	66.66	15.38	Yes	63 [18]
Minnesota New Country School: 6 thru 12: 108	All	37.25	67.21	57.69	Yes	30 [33]
Naytahwaush Community School: K thru 6: 101	All	34.69	40	0	Yes	95 [31]
Nerstrand Charter School: K thru 5: 153	All	69.23	80.76	53.84	Yes	18 [12]
New Century Charter School: 7 thru 12: 144	All	28.12	47.12	25	No	42 [19]
Northern Lights Community School: 6 thru 12: 97	All	9.3	16.07	5.88	No	71 [30]
River Heights Charter School: 9 thru 12: 69	All	**	46.66	10	No	9 [13]
Riverbend Academy: 6 thru 12: 69	All	19.23	65.21	30	No	57 [51]
Sage Charter Academy: 9 thru 12: 86	All	4.76	28.57	11.11	Yes	66 [22]

** too few students to calculate. [FRL]=Free or reduced price lunch; [SE]=Special Education
Source: http://education.state.mn.us (Accessed, Aug. 31, 2010).

The demographics of the teacher-run schools vary substantially. Throughout Minnesota, 36 percent of students come from families with incomes low enough to qualify for a free-or-reduced-price lunch. The teacher-run schools range between 9 and

89 percent. But the teacher-run schools generally enroll much larger percentages of special education students. Avalon, for example, has 45 percent more special education students than the state average, and Minnesota New Country enrolls special education students at 2.5 times the state average. Anecdotal evidence from observers of these schools, suggest that parents of special education students choose the teacher-run schools because their children seem to thrive there, like school more, and stay engaged.

The Milwaukee teacher-run schools test scores approximated those of the city and were substantially lower than the state as a whole. The demographics of the teacher-run schools were also closer to those of the city, where 15 percent of the students are white, compared to the state, where

76 percent are. The teacher-run schools also mirror the city's overall measure of students in poverty, over 75 percent.

The range of test score results among the teacher-run schools is very large, and so is the student population served. The percentage of free or reduced price lunch eligible students ranges from 31 to 92 percent; the percentage of second language learners from zero to 58 percent. The percentage of African-American students ranges from 1 to 96 percent; that of Latino students from 2 to 99 percent. These data underscore the difficulty of using single measure test scores as a means of evaluating the schools, but it also underscores the need for the schools to develop their own measures, built on the school's own objectives and their distinctive characteristics, an issue discussed in a later section. In addition to test scores, there are other indicators of academic progress. The schools appear to have better than average college test results and college-going rates. The EdVisions schools averaged 23.6 on the ACT compared to a national average of 21.2. The SAT for students from these schools was 1749 compared to a national average of 1518. Over 82 percent of EdVisions graduates went on to two- or four- year colleges, compared to a national average of 68 percent (Farris-Berg, 2010).

Milwaukee Teacher Run School Test Score Results, 2009

	Reading: Proficient or Above	Math: Proficient or Above	Free/Reduced Lunch: Students Qualifying	Special Education Students
Wisconsin	81.5%	77.3%	37%	14%
Milwaukee	58.9%	50.8%	79%	19%
Mean of Teacher-Run Schools	55.6%	38.9%	76%	20%

Mark Van Ryzin at Education Evolving linked psychometric measurement to the notion of hope, and over the last six years the Hope Study has tracked a measurement of hope (Richard Snyder's Dispositional Hope Scale) (Van Ryzin, 2009). Students with high Hope Scale scores believe that they have the ability to find workable routes to their goals and that they can meet them. The longer students are at Avalon or the EdVisons schools, the better they feel about their futures. Measurements of autonomy, belongingness, and competency plus academic press (questions such as "My teachers press me to do thoughtful work") are related to increased student engagement, and that drives both increased academic performance and an increase in the Hope Scale measurement. Interestingly, the idea of mastery—trying hard and understanding—that is encouraged at Avalon is positively linked to student engagement and results. But the idea of performance for its own sake and sparse rewards is negatively linked. The average student in an EdVisions school will grow on the Hope Scale from about 48, which is the national average, to over 55 in six years.

The Hope Study is not likely to replace state standardized tests. But it speaks to a willingness of these schools to put their values into measurable terms and to track them over time.

The policy dimension: Islands or a network of practice

The question of whether cooperatives can work in public education requires a complex answer. The Minnesota experiment appears to have settled the teacher financial ownership question in the negative. The notion of a for- profit cooperative se ling services to a school district, appears not to be growing. Most of the teachers associated with the rural Minnesota schools, where the EdVisions cooperative started, are associate members, essentially employees, instead of partners in the cooperative itself. And most pointedly, there are not a lot of profits to share. EdVisions reported passing out $100-$300 bonuses some years back, but that level of incentive is not going to attract would-be venture capitalists to teaching.

However, the idea of teachers as owners of their work and self-managers appears poised for growth, and it is coincident with older labor traditions associated with craft and artistry (Kerchner, 2003). Interest in teacher-run schools is growing among teacher unions, and a union-backed teacher-run school is due to open in Detroit in fall 2010 (Walsh-Sarnecki, 2010).

If one were to ask whether teacher cooperatives are about to replace school district hierarchies, the answer would be "of course not." But if one were to ask whether it is possible for groups of teachers to run successful schools on their own and in the process increase the degrees of autonomy and flexibility in their own jobs, then one would get a different answer. Yes, it is possible, and it would be easier if public policy would better enable teacher-run schools. And if one were to ask whether there are lessons to be learned from these cooperatives about how we might redesign teaching as work and schools as learning organizations, then many possibilities flow.

Coherence though collaboration

The value of a single point of authority has been raised to the status of civil religion in business-oriented school reform quarters. Stand-up mayors and big talking, brash superintendents are in fashion. But experts need wide latitude in their work, or as Peter Drucker noted, "knowledge workers can't be managed" at least not in the command and control manner (Drucker, 1993, p. 65). Expert workers, in whatever form of organization, challenge the notion that one gains coherence through compliance with a set of rules or procedures designed outside of the immediate workplace. From work rules about the length of faculty meetings or the school day to a curriculum pacing plan that mandates the number of minutes spent on a lesson, the notion of expert teacher judgment clashes with the view that coherence in the system can only be provided by a hierarchy topped with someone with unquestioned authority.

Teacher-run schools try to create coherence through other means, and are therefore good case examples of the practices that would have to be imported into district schools if types of autonomous schools, such as the Pilot Schools, were to thrive. As such, they create a few imperatives.

A different division of labor

First, and most obviously, teacher-run schools have a much different division of labor than conventional schools. Adult roles are more diffuse and much less specialized. There are relatively more teachers engaged in the core academic subjects and fewer ancillary personnel. There are more shared responsibilities, and less demarcation of duties with specific work positions. There is more fluidity in moving responsibility from one person to another.

Yet, the most common belief is that teacher-run schools are neither possible on any but a trivial scale, nor are they desirable. Newspaper stories about the founding of a teacher-run school in New Jersey drew disbelieving comments. James Lytle, a professor at the University of Pennsylvania questioned whether teachers have the patience to do the 'adminis-trivia.' And Michael Petri li of the Thomas B. Fordham Institute offered the opinion that only a handful of teachers could pull off such an audacious organizational feat (Hu, 2010).

These comments — pulled from context as are most newspaper quotes — miss the essential point about the division of labor inherent in teacher-led schools. A lot of what teachers do at Avalon, which would be called administrative work at a conventional school, is rather seamlessly wrapped into daily activities. A teacher and other students, rather than an assistant principal, deals with discipline. A teacher, rather than a classified worker, observes the lunch line. A teacher, rather than a chain of office workers and administrators, talks with parents when they call. Teacher-run schools are not regular schools in which the tasks have been shuffled; they are schools where tasks are done differently. Some of the things that teachers do in regular high schools — master scheduling, for example — virtually disappear because the project-based nature of the schools means that time is used differently.

If one were to examine doing tasks differently in a careful and deliberate manner, in much more depth than this study was able, one would find implications for productivity in public education. For example, the economic production function of a lesson is different when students inquire into needed facts than when a teacher dishes them out in a lecture. The cost of individualized instruction is different in a project mode than when a teacher is charged with the responsibility of individualizing lessons. The cost of discipline differs when a student mediation team handles the problem than it is when an assistant principal does the same job. For decades, it has been claimed that school reforms don't change the core function of teaching and learning. These teacher-run schools appear to be an exception to that rule.

The critique of teacher-run schools also notes that their faculty need a broader skill set than most teachers, and that is very much the case. They do need to understand budgets, not the arcaneness of fund accounting, but the fundamentals of what a school's income and outflows are and what causes them. Understanding economic reality in a teacher-run school creates competence in putting together a learning system that works, is attractive to students and their parents, and is kind to teachers and their time. Teachers also need more skills in dealing with parents. Parents come to schools like Avalon because they are watchful of their children's education, and sometimes managing these expectations is difficult, as is the case in a private school or other charter school that is dependent on a continued flow of students seeking the school. Angry or questioning parents can't just be referred to an administrative flack catcher. However, these same parents are also central to the learning system. They sign off on student projects and often serve as resources in their completion. And they become the school's most loyal advocates.

Unitary democracy instead of central authority

The second distinguishing feature of teacher-run schools that would have to be carried into district schools in a Pilot or similar model is the substitution of unitary democracy for central authority (Mansbridge, 1990)(Bryk & Schneider, 2002). They rely on strong cultures, a common mission, and relational trust. The idea of unitary democracy, as opposed to interest group democracy or political parties, makes the goals of the cooperative enterprise more important than those of individual positions. These schools are not the refuge of iconoclasts. For schools like Avalon, New Country, or SUPAR to work, the adults who work in them need to create decisional norms that come to conclusions quickly and avoid the "process paralysis" associated with past attempts at school-site decision-making. At Avalon, faculty use a "Fist of Five" voting system indicating how supportive of a proposal they are. A closed fist blocks action, but a person who does this is required to articulate an acceptable alternative. In practice, there are not a lot of closed fists.

The lack of deep disagreement is in part a matter of socialization. There has been a lot of stability among the teaching ranks at Avalon, and at some of the other teacher-run schools, but where there hasn't been, the organizations are struggling. And the lack of deep disagreement is partly a function of an evaluation system that can remove people who "don't understand how we do things here." Staff learn to work at Avalon by being assigned a mentor in their first year, and they are paired with an experienced teacher in the same advisory space. Thus, every new teacher gets two support personnel. (Compare this level of support with the sink-or-swim initiation found in many district run schools.) Also, Avalon uses a 360-degree evaluation system in which everyone evaluates everyone. But more than having the structure of the evaluation system in place, the school has a culture that requires it to be used clinically. At Avalon, the teachers who have not had their

contracts renewed were largely those who did not want to teach within that school's culture of project-based pedagogy.

In behavioral terms, the cooperatives substitute norms of reciprocity, civility, and engagement for those of obedience and rule following. Disengagement threatens a cooperative, just as insubordination threatens hierarchy. There are clear examples within Avalon and the other cooperatives of disengaged teachers, but the system will not tolerate many of them, and the process of annual evaluations where the last question is whether this person should return to the school next year creates a situation in which even senior faculty members cannot rely on past years of attentiveness to secure themselves a continuing position. "I paid my dues when I was younger," does not create a claim on a job.

But collaboration also has a steely edge. Anna Wesley has been associated with Avalon almost since its founding. She was a student intern at the school and later returned to teach in the middle school. She has been on the personnel committee for years. The committee has a number of routine jobs, including the annual evaluation system, and it also deals with complaints and disputes among faculty members in the same manner as the mediation system works among students. But it also has to be willing to confront instances of bad behavior or poor teaching. This happened several times, including last year when an experienced teacher was told that he would not be rehired.

As in the practice of peer review in traditional school districts, the personnel function at Avalon and the other teacher-run schools depends on the ability and willingness of teachers to "call the question" in situations where the welfare of the school requires that another teacher be removed from his or her job (Koppich, Asher, & Kerchner, 2002). This process requires behaviors far different than those expected in a traditional district school, where discipline and discharge decisions are encased in a bureaucracy. It is not that there is no due process at Avalon. There are disciplinary steps, interventions, and action plans, just as there are in a conventional school district. But at the end of the decisional chain, teachers will decide.

"It is not easy being a member of the personnel committee," Wesley notes. Teachers have a very close working relationship, and frequently they socialize with one another on the weekends. So, when someone approaches her with a gripe or complaint, she has to ask, "Why are you telling me this?" Is it just venting about a tough day or an irritating situation, or do you want the school to counsel, investigate, or take action? Unitary democracy is not just a matter of discussing things until everyone is comfortable with everything; it's about running an effective school.

Introspective routines

Third, teacher-run schools develop introspective routines that cause both students and adults to inquire deeply into whether and how learning is taking place. These are brilliant when they succeed and delusional when they do not. Field research provides evidence of both. At Avalon, teachers review student achievement annually and report on their data to their charter sponsor, Hamline University. Teachers set goals for the following year. In 2009, it was to pay special attention to students who scored in the bottom 25 percent in reading growth (Bakken, 2010). Avalon, like many schools, uses a rubric to score student work. But at Avalon, unlike most schools, the rubric is built into the routines, so that a student needs to use the rubric to reflect on his or her projects. Faculty use the rubric to give feedback. Students use the rubric in finding ways to improve and resubmit projects. Yet, the routines for using student work to consciously question how project teaching could be stronger — how more expert projects could be produced — seem underdeveloped. "We are getting better at using data to change our practices, but, again, we question how useful tests are with such a small sample size. We try to focus less on the numbers and more on the individuals. It is important to get them reading complicated materials," said Bakken (2010).

Project-based pedagogy

Fourth, these teacher-run schools all teach using projects as the main pedagogy, although there are some schools where the project-based identity is being compromised by a retreat to class teaching that better fits with the conventional "grammar of schooling." Bundling projects and a flat organizational structure fundamentally changes the role of teachers as workers and instructors. Students become the workers in this system, not the teachers. If a student isn't getting work done, the project method doesn't say to the faculty member, "Teach harder." The project method moves the responsibility for creating projects and keeping on pace to their completion to the student. The students I talked to at Avalon and other project-based schools were quick to tell me that the management of their time and effort was one of their key practical lessons. "I am a sophomore," said one student, "I should be a junior. I'm behind in my work because I hung out with the wrong people last year. This year's different, and I am catching up."

The most obvious lesson to draw from Avalon and the other teacher-run schools is that students are capable of much more self-control than most schools expect of them. While there are many reasons that urban high schools appear to be just on the ragged edge of anarchy, organizing student life around external control rather than student self-control is counterproductive. It directs resources to control that would be better spent on learning and teaching. And it fails to teach important 21st Century skills of self-control, collaboration, and solving hard-to-define problems.

There is a parallel lesson for adults: faculty and staff are much more capable of designing their own work and of understanding changing circumstances than the traditional practice of school administration through command and control would suggest. But to move from a compliance model to a cooperative model requires a great deal of craft effort on the part of the adults designing and starting up the school.

A cooperative enterprise is not simply a place where individual teachers work as they wish. In fact, historically, there was more room for individuals to hide out in conventional bureaucracies. Shielded by the classroom door, the lack of supervision, and the union contract, teachers often gained substantial operating independence so long as they did not disobey direct orders or challenge superiors. In a teacher-run cooperative, the obligation for joint action is imperative. Teachers have to understand the relationship between "my job" and how the curriculum of the school works, how resources are deployed.

Successfully managing paradox

Education reform is generally hampered by excess of ideology, and the almost immediate classification of any project as either socially progressive or market conservative. Teacher-run schools successfully manage the paradox of borrowing from, and in some ways appealing to, both camps. It is the management of paradox mentioned at the outset of this study that makes teacher-run schools worthy of further investment and policy attention.

The workers' cooperative, of course, has roots in utopian socialism, and the argument for linking workers with control of their tools is captured in critiques of the capitalist mode of production (Braverman, 1974). At the same time, the idea of teacher cooperatives appeals to those of American Enterprise Association entrepreneurial stripe, who would argue that the substantive problem of public education lies in the bureaucratic underbrush and the lack of ability for people who want to try novel and interesting approaches to do so (Hess, 2010).

Teacher-run schools manage the paradox between these two camps because they recognize and organize around the fact that schools are inherently both formal organizations and small communities. The formal organization aspect of teacher-run schools recognizes that there are specific goals, that the organization has to be maintained, and that discipline and authority are part of the process. But control is based on shared understanding and responsibility rather than hierarchy. The small community aspect of these schools recognizes the aspect of schooling that public policy often misses: Schools are at their best when they are transformative for students and teachers, and that "the daily life of the community shapes, sometimes in very subtle ways, the kinds of persons students become (Bryk & Hermanson, 1993, p. 454)."

The argument for teacher-run schools derives in part from a desire to create better jobs for teachers, jobs that would broaden the talent pool of people eager to take up teaching and willing to take on more responsibility than civil servants are required or a lowed to. These teachers take on more economic risk than a conventional public school teacher. If the teacher-run school fails, their jobs go with them. Except for the limited retreat rights in the Milwaukee setting, there is no soft landing position.

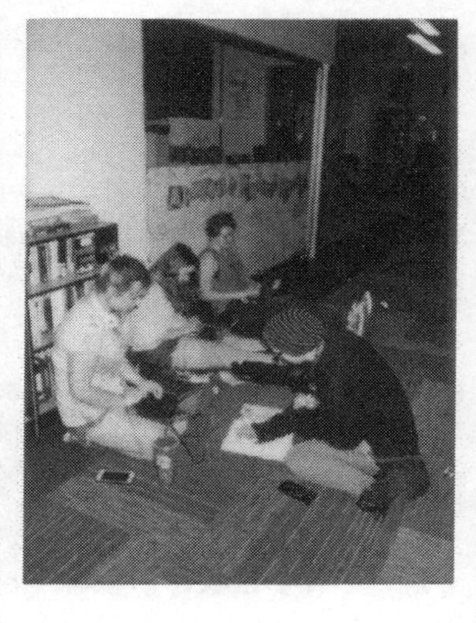

At the same time, there seems to be less faculty churning and less chafing against authority than in the typical management- driven charter school, some of which have business plans that depend on a constant replacement of younger teachers. Thus, we find the working paradox of people willingly signing up for harder jobs with less economic protection but more control over the content of their work. Clearly, not everyone who goes into teaching is willing to accept this bargain, but those who do find the rewards of controlling their own jobs to be a good trade.

Teacher-run schools also reveal an interesting paradox about achievement. They are subject to the same test score accountability as teachers in district schools, and because the schools are for the most part charters subject to decisions about renewal, they are on a shorter accountability leash than most district schools. At the same time, there is a clear belief that the goal of their schools is not to produce higher test scores. Theirs is a broader curriculum in which measured cognitive achievement is subordinated by important student skills in solving problems, in personal discipline, and self-control. The existence of these managed paradoxes suggests that teacher-run schools are a useful experiment on their own and that finding policies that extract the important lessons about school practice is a worthwhile undertaking.

Finding policy levers

Two types of public policy instruments are necessary to support the founding and operation of teacher-run schools. The policy mechanisms for creating teacher-run schools that bundle project-based learning and student-as-worker-and-citizen with a workers' cooperative are already known and in place. It is the mechanisms for building the educative capacity of these schools that are severely underdeveloped.

Policy that establishes teacher-run schools

We know what is required in public policy to create a teacher-run school: get autonomy and money to the schools. The experiments with school site management that sprouted in the 1980s and 1990s foundered largely on the inability of school districts to devolve sufficient authority to schools so that the people involved in them were willing to keep working at the process. When there were relatively few substantive decisions to make, teachers and school administrators in so-called site- managed schools fell back on protracted arguments about decisional process and ultimately became burned out and disillusioned.

Thus, it is of little surprise that most of the existing teacher-run schools use charter school laws to legitimate their governance and finance. Charter laws are well suited to this purpose, and they appear to work well to a low groups of teachers who want to form schools to do so. In addition, there are two emerging structures that could also be used to a low and encourage teacher-run schools in existing school districts.

In 2009 Minnesota authorized "site governed schools,"

essentially in-district charter schools but where school boards authorize them and teachers remain employees of the district and members of the same bargaining unit as those in conventional schools. There were two ideas behind the legislation. First, districts needed some of the flexibility found in the charter sector. Second, innovative arrangements needed an anchor in statute so that the granting of rights to a group of teachers to form a school would not depend on continuity in leadership of a school district. It is too early to know the effects of the law: whether school districts will use it to set up internal innovation labs or whether the cultural imprint of traditional public schools is so strong that innovation from within will not persist. In fall 2010 the Minneapolis Public Schools will open the first teacher-run school using the new statute: a French immersion school.

Teacher-run schools have also been founded through the Pilot School model, another form of in-district charters that was founded in the Boston Public Schools and which has migrated to the Los Angeles Unified School District (LAUSD) and other locations. Rather than relying on legislation as their source of legitimacy, the 21 Boston Pilot Schools, which now enroll 9,000 students, are the creation of a collective bargaining contract between the Boston Teachers Union and the school district. LAUSD has 10 operating Pilot Schools and 10 more are due to start in 2010. A traditional public school in Denver has converted to Pilot Status and a teacher-led school is starting in Detroit (Khadaroo, 2010).

The Pilot School experiment has been sufficiently long running to have both substantial operational evidence and an ebb-and- flow political history (Pearlman, 2000). As was the intent of the Minnesota law, Pilot Schools were formed explicitly to serve as research and development sites. Only a few of the pilots are teacher-run in the sense that Avalon is, but all of them have autonomy over budget, staffing, operational governance, curriculum and assessment, and the school calendar.

For example, teachers voluntarily choose to work at Pilot Schools and sign an "election-to-work-agreement" that contains the working conditions that will pertain to that school in the coming year. That agreement is revised annually (French, 2006). The school governing boards have a great deal of autonomy, but working through the budget process with the school district has been historically difficult.

Although not all the Pilot Schools are teacher-run, that form or governance has generated its own support mechanism, much as EdVisions has. In Boston, the non- profit Center for Collaborative Education (CCE) acts as coach, trainer, evaluator, and advocate for the pilots. It has also assisted the schools in Los Angeles. That city is also developing its own Pilot School development organization, an outgrowth of a compact between the city's labor organizations, the school district, United Way, the Chamber of Commerce, the city, and surrounding colleges and universities.

A 'text' to develop and improve teacher-run schools

The second needed policy instruments are those necessary to support the development and improvement of teacher-run schools. Although EdVisions and CCE exist as supports for teacher-run schools, the infrastructure for developing their operations and training their personnel remains underdeveloped. As Thomas Kuhn (1970) wrote 40 years ago, one way of telling whether a paradigm shift has taken place is to see if anyone has written a text about the new idea. The schools such as Avalon need a text.

They need a text so that others can follow their ideas. Simply structuring a school as autonomous does not provide instruction in its operation, and, indeed, the lack of organizational guidance for schools that are organizationally innovative may explain why most charter schools look a great deal like conventional schools and why the charter school movement has proven to be a disappointment for those who thought it would be a source of great innovation.

A text is not simply a book, although it might be that in part. It might be a series of pamphlets, a web site, a series of apps for a handheld computer, summer conferences, a virtual reality experience, or all of those things. The text is a guide to practice, that says, in effect, that if one believes in the bundle of ideas that constitute Avalon and similar schools, here's how to put those ideas into action. It takes the ideals of Education Evolving and EdVisions and creates a coherent vision of practice.

The first function of a text would be as an organizing manual. Public education has done this before: in the work of the administrative progressives to organize school districts early in the 20th century and more recently in the most successful union organizing campaign in a half-century. In both cases, there were both organizers who did the work and a text on how to do it. The primary union text of the period was not hard bound, but held together with post binders so that new pages could be inserted as experience warranted (Wollett & Chanin, 1974).

If teacher-run schools are to thrive and grow, it is extremely important that they have an organizing mechanism, just as it has been to the charter school movement. By definition, teacher-run schools are not scalable in the same way that bureaucracies are, and scalability and growth are chronic problems of cooperative organizations outside of education. Charter management organizations are unlikely to take up the banner of teacher-run schools, and the concept is still alien to school districts and most teacher unions. So, it is extremely important that the mavericks and visionaries who are intrigued by the idea have a network of knowledge and process to follow.

The text would also serve as a training manual. In hundreds of teacher education programs throughout the country, teachers are trained to work in bureaucracies. There is no teacher education program for teachers who want to run their own schools. As even the short descriptions contained in this case study illustrate, these teachers have quite different occupational lives than those in conventional schools, and they need practical guidance in how to take on those roles. They need to be able to mate higher order concepts, such as democratic schooling, with the practicality of getting rowdy, pubescent junior high school students to understand how to express disagreement in productive ways. They need to get teachers with communitarian instincts to understand budgeting, forecasting, and planning. They need to get those who want to nurture students to link their instruction to high standards.

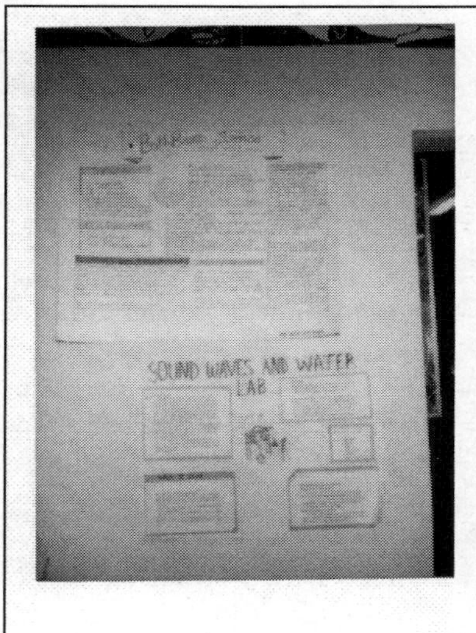

As in any start-up, the first wave of teacher-run schools has been the product of true believers who were willing to treat their own lives as vocations and occupations as an experiment. They put in ridiculous numbers of hours to create productive relationships with one another and to learn the craft skills of leadership, and of followership, which is in many ways more difficult. And while it is the case that each new school will have to found itself as a community, later adopters should benefit from accumulated knowledge of practice.

There are good historical data on how training programs for non-standard schools work and don't, and there are currently running experiments in organizational settings as diverse as High Tech High in San Diego, California, which runs its own graduate school, to Teach for America, which operates its own training programs.

Finally, a text would create routines. These a low teachers and students to learn from their daily experiences that make them better at their jobs and the schools smarter as organizations. Schools, such as Avalon, are well structured to avoid the problem of that Peter Senge (2000) calls "organizational learning disability," and to become smart, continuously improving organizations. The project creation and reflection format, and the use of a rubric for evaluation lends themselves to organizational knowledge co lection with every student undertaking. Yet, because the schools are small, and their operations unbureaucratic, much of this knowledge is tacit. It needs to be made explicit, captured, written down, passed along.

The schools also need routines to deal with their data. Schools such as Avalon have a particularly hard time dealing with the official numbers, state test score data, and the like. They are willing to use positive results as evidence that they are achieving, but there is a fundamental belief that these indicators are not worth much. Student results, such as the SAT, have high consequences for students and may lead to favorable comparisons, but they don't help the schools learn.

These schools could benefit from building a data pyramid: a set of high-level indicators at the top, based on the best quantifiable information that the schools feel represent their values and goals, and a set of much more behavioral, authentic indicators at the bottom. It is important that this network of schools make these indicators explicit (Bryk & Hermanson, 1993). Otherwise, they will be judged only by test score results or the data other observers choose.

These schools already engage in a practice that, with a little augmentation, would raise their student's work to the level of a public indicator. Each project-based school I visited used exhibitions as a means for students to display and explain their work to peers and advisors. The aggregate of these individual displays is a school-wide exhibition that provides exemplars posted on the school's web site and available for public inspection along with, data on the numbers of projects completed and the rankings projects received.

At the second level of the pyramid, schools would collect data about themselves, much as Avalon now does for its annual reports to its charter school sponsor, and also more private data for use inside the school itself. For example, Avalon can boast a 96 percent graduation rate, and relatively few discipline issues, but these data are not part of the state's report. Its projects are on public view during Presentation Nights, that have been attended by 150 observers during the year (Avalon School, 2008).

At the third level of the pyramid — classrooms or advisories as they are called at Avalon — these schools produce very rich data, most of it qualitative. These data are often the most insightful, but it is often not caught and fed back into the school. These schools need routines to collect and analyze school and classroom data just as conventional district schools do. For example, engagement is a huge indicator of whether students are getting on with their projects. Teachers and students have to be able to discern when apparent idleness and playfulness is time necessary for the creative aspects of a project to come together and when it is goofing off or work avoidance. Understanding the right balance, and making that knowledge explicit is a big part of making project-based learning effective and efficient.

However, finding the policy levers to build institutional capacity around teacher-run schools will not be an easy or straightforward task. Where is it costless for a legislature to give teachers permission to start a school, it costs money to provide the infrastructure, what we are calling the text, for them to develop and improve. In these fiscal times, the teacher-run schools are up against substantial reluctance to raise new tax revenue and the hoarding of resources by existing schools.

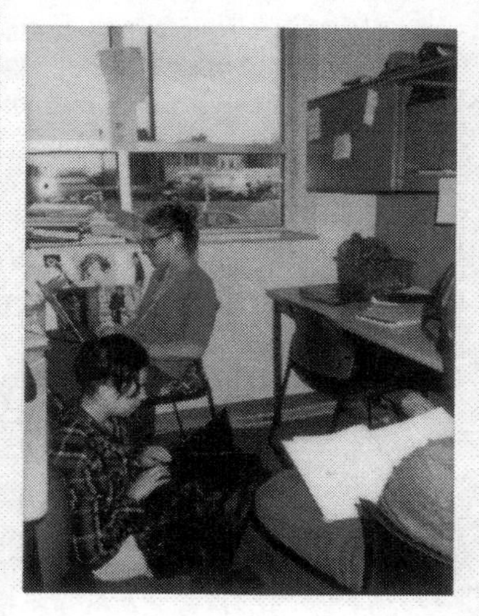

Private philanthropy could provide the venture funding to better document what has gone on in these schools. It could underwrite teacher training and professional development, as it has in the academies run by Teach For America and the graduate school run by High Tech High in San Diego. But this would require a level of commitment higher than that which these schools have received in the past.

The more open-ended but difficult source of policy leverage rests with public school coalition partners. The bundled model of teacher-run schools, as represented in Avalon and the EdVisions schools, will be difficult to replicate outside the charter sector unless there is a strong champion for it within the existing public school establishment. Teacher unions are the most likely candidates for this role, but to date they have done more sniffing around the edges rather than actively engaging the idea.

The Pilot School model has become attractive to unions who themselves seek flexibility or who fear the encroachment of charter schools into the district's enrollment. The politics for developing this model are at their most visible in Los Angeles, where the Public School Choice Initiative, begun in the summer of 2009, subjects newly constructed schools and those whose performance has lagged for years to a request-for-proposal process in which various would-be school operators present alternate designs for school management and operation.

The advantage to linking the teacher-run schools with teacher unions lies in the union contract and its capacity to influence the flows of school and district funds. The disadvantage is that most teacher unionists have, ironically, preserved the large scale public bureaucracy — the very thing that they organized against — as the last best expression of an idealized public sector. So, Pilot Schools, and any deviation for the current model, are distrusted. Substantial, and I suspect prolonged, political coalition building will be required.

A second policy lever can be found in teacher education, where the requirements for certification could be tweaked in ways that made it attractive to a hardy few universities to offer specializations in teacher licensure to those teachers who wanted to work in teacher-run schools. This would a low the normal flows of tuition and state support to help establish teacher-training programs.

The third policy lever lies in the unbundling of ideas. There are more project-based schools than there are teacher-run schools, for example, and the idea of building schooling around a connection between head and hands is gaining broader attention than that of teacher professional partnerships. States, and the technology industry, are much interested in the developments of pedagogy that breaks down the old batch process mode of learning regardless of whether the schools involved are teacher-run or operated as conventional hierarchies. Much of the text for school improvement, and semi-autonomous school organization could take place within a coalition of organizations interested in pedagogy.

Likewise, there is a broader coalition of people and organizations interested in self-management than those in education. Grass roots community based organizations, small non-governmental organizations operating in developing countries, a large league of cooperatives in the United States, operate on non-hierarchical or hybrid organizational styles. These are genuinely interesting, and have captured the attention of people who study organizations for decades. If one thinks of teacher- run schools as a special case of cellular organizations, then planning an infrastructure that causes them to spread and thrive connects with a well-known and developed research base.

The Bottom Line

Avalon and its sister schools exist on wonderful islands. It may be enough that they are refuges from the storms that have engulfed American public education. But there are larger lessons to be learned from them. If the claims that teacher-run schools are a valuable alternative to the national policy dialogue are to be made with much vigor, then much more needs to be done to capture the craft knowledge of Avalon and similar schools, to make it available to those who would want to start them, and to apply clinical knowledge to school improvement among them. This, along with necessary policy intervention, is the bridge between the islands of teacher-run schools and the causeway to the mainland.

References

Associated Press. "New Wis. Law Targets Failing Public Schools." April 30 2010. Avalon School, "Peer Mediation and Restorative Justice Manual." p 11.

Avalon School. Avalon School: Passion for Learning: Annual Report 2007-2008. St. Paul, MN: Author, 2008, p. 12. Bakken, Carrie, personal communication, 2010.

Braverman, Harry. Labor and Monopoly Capital. New York: Monthly Review Press, 1974.

Bryk, Anthony S. and Barbara Schneider. "Relational Trust." In Trust in Schools: A Core Resource for Improvement, New York, NY: Russe l Sage Foundation, 2002.

Bryk, Anthony S., and Hermanson, Kim L. "Educational Indicator Systems: Observations on Their Structure, Interpretation and Use." Review of Research in Education 19 (1993): 451-84, at 454.

Drucker, Peter F. Post-Capitalist Society. New York: Harper Collins, 1993: 65. Farris-Berg, Kim. Personal correspondence, May 2010.

French, Dan. "Boston's Pilot Schools: Progress and Promise in Urban School Reform." Education Week, April 19, 2006, 33-34.

Gabriel, Trip. 2010. Despite Push, Success At Charter Schools is Mixed. http://nytimes.com/2010/05/02charters.html.

Hawkins, Beth. 2010. Teacher Gets to Tout St. Paul's Avalon Co-Op School to Nation's Top Education Officials. http://www.minnpost.com/stories/2010/07/01/19375.

Hess, Frederick M. Education Unbound: The Promise and Practice of Greenfield Schooling. Alexandria, VA: ASCD, 2010. Hu, Winnie. 2010. In a New Role, Teachers Move to Run Schools.

Ingersoll, Richard M. "Short on Power, Long on Responsibility." Educational Leadership 65, no. 1 (2007): 20-25.

Kerchner, Charles Taylor. "The Modern Guild: The Prospects for Organizing Around Quality in Public Education." In Transforming Unions: edited by Jon Brock, and David Lipsky, Urbana, IL: University of Illinois Press, 2003.

Khadaroo, Stacy. 2010. School Teachers in Charge? Why Some Schools Are Forgoing Principals. http://www.csmonitor.com/USA/Education/2010/0901/School-teachers-in-charge-Why-some-schools-are-forgoing-principals (accessed Sept. 13, 2010).

Koppich, Julia, Carla Asher, and Charles Kerchner. Developing Careers, Building a Profession: The Rochester Career in Teaching Plan. New York: National Commission on Teaching & America's Future, 2002.

Kuhn, Thomas S. The Structure of Scientific Revolutions. Chicago: University of Chicago Press, 1970.

Mansbridge, Jane. "The Rise and Fall of Self-Interest in the Explanation of Political Life." In Beyond Self-Interest, edited by Jane Mansbridge, 3-24. Chicago: University of Chicago Press, 1990.

Nelson, William, and Judy Ziewzcz. "Forward." In Cooperation Works!: How People Are Using Cooperative Action to Rebuild Communities and Revitalize the Economy, 1-6. Rochester, MN: Lone Oak Press, 1996, p. 5.

Newell, Ronald J., and Van Ryzin, Mark J. "Growing Hope as a Determinant of School Effectiveness." Phi Delta Kappan 88 (2007): 465-71: 466.

Pearlman, Bob. "Smarter Charters? Creating Boston's Pilot Schools." In Creating New Schools: How Small Schools Are Changing American Education, edited by Evin Cinchy, 38-45. Teachers College Press, 2000.

Rofes, Eric. ND. Teachers and Communitarians: A Charter School Cooperative in Rural Minnesota, p. 10. http://www.ericrofes.com/research/Teachers_Communitarians_wc.doc.pdf (accessed May 17, 2010).

Senge, Peter. "The Industrial Age System of Education." In Schools That Learn, edited by Peter Senge, Nelda Cambron-McCabe, Timothy Lucas, Bryan Smith, Janis Dutton, and Art Kleiner, New York: Doubleday, 2000.

Stone, Deborah. Policy Paradox: The Art of Political Decision Making. New York: W.W. Norton, 1998. The Constitution of the School of Avalon, Law 13, October 2009.

Thomas, Doug, Walter Enloe, and Ron Newell, (eds.) The Coolest School in America: How Small Learning Communities Are Changing Everything. Lanham, MD: Scarecrow Education, 2005.

Van Ryzin, Mark J. "Measuring School Capacity for Positive Youth Development." Unpublished manuscript (2009).

Walsh-Sarnecki, Peggy. 2010. Detroit Public Schools Tries Something New: A School Run By Teachers. http://www.freep.com/article/20100708/NEWS01/7080367/Detroit-Public-Schools- tries-something-new-A-school- run-by-teachers (accessed July 30, 2010).

Ward, Kevin. "Avalon Book Chapter." unpublished manuscript (2007): p. 11.

Wollett, Donald H., and Robert H. Chanin. The Law and Practice of Teacher Negotiations. Washington, D.C.: The Bureau of National Affairs, Inc, 1974.

Wollmering, Pat, "Anna Interview Report," Hamline University, 2008, pp. 3, 11.

Chapter 12

Giving Students Ownership of Learning

Ronald J. Newell and Walter Enloe

An innovative model now operating in 47 schools puts student-created projects at the center of the high school curriculum. What is 1 + 2 + 4 + (6 × 180 × 13)? Answer: E. This equation suggests that 1 classroom teacher, using content between the 2 covers of a book, within the 4 wa ls of a classroom, for 6 hours a day, for 180 days a year, for 13 years, equals an education.

Unfortunately, this model is based on faulty assumptions: that time is the constant and learning is the variable; that knowledge is easily divided into discrete disciplines that should be taught as separate entities; that students must be led by the experts in those disciplines; and that young people will not learn unless adults control the environment.

Today, a number of charter schools have challenged those assumptions using an innovative model developed at the Minnesota New Country School in Henderson, Minnesota. The school's founders created a radica ly different format for education — one based on the belief that students can take charge of their own learning, working with advisor-teachers who help them gain the necessary knowledge and skills. The school's personalized program in grades 7-12 enables each student, with input from teaching staff, parents, and other practitioners, to design projects that fulfill state curriculum standards. The format does away with classes, classrooms, be ls, mandatory textbooks, teacher lectures, most testing, teacher lesson plans, and student competition for grades.

In 2000, the Bill and Melinda Gates Foundation funded EdVisions Schools, an organization dedicated to replicating the Minnesota New Country School model. To date, 47 schools have adopted the model. We know that high schools can and do work when they break the mold.

Components of the Model

Let's look at how the EdVisions model facilitates the work of youth as self-directed producers and learners; connects with students; ensures that students are achieving the intended results; and engages all stakeholders, including teachers, in learning.

Creating Self-Directed Learners

The leading form of learning in EdVisions schools is self-directed, project-based learning. On the basis of their interests and academic needs, students generate and complete individual or group projects. To facilitate this kind of learning, each student has a personal work space that has an Internet-accessible computer as well as access to printers and other media production technology. The following examples give an idea of the infinite variety of projects.

After hearing her advisor talk about the book Lies My Teacher Told Me: Everything Your American History Book Got Wrong, by James W. Loewen (New Press, 2008), Emily did a project comparing the information found in this book with the information presented in other U.S. history books. She created a slide show that compared texts and showed differences in the ways books interpreted many historical events. She gave her slide show at presentation night and was also invited to present it to a Charter School Symposium at Hamline University in Saint Paul, Minnesota. Her project fulfilled state curriculum standards both in American history and American literature.

Brooke did a junior project on factory farming and slaughterhouses. She got the idea for the project after she began questioning whether vegetarianism was a legitimate way to stay healthy. The project grew from her investigation of antibodies and hormones in meat products to a history of husbandry and slaughtering techniques. She also investigated laws governing the U.S. meat industry and compared them with those in other countries. She wrote a major research paper that she will use in her portfolio for college entrance and scholarship applications.

She also created a visual presentation and exhibit, using samples of vegetable sources of protein, examples of chemicals used in raising meat, and photos of slaughterhouse practices. Her project met standards in biology, environmental science, history, and civics.

Hannah has an interest in music and became acquainted with classical compositions while listening to varieties of music. She did a project on classical composers, primarily Mozart and Beethoven. Her project covered the history of musical composition, the backgrounds of the composers, influences on their lives, and so on. As she learned about the Mozart Effect—the theory that listening to classical music enhances child development and learning—she became interested in the psychology and genius of the composers. Her products were two research papers and an exhibit with pictures and time lines. She met standards in music appreciation and history.

Hannah also teamed with a friend to do a project called The Science of Dreaming. As they discussed questions about their own dreams and interacted with other teens who had similar questions, Hannah and Amber decided to discover how and why dreams occur. They started by studying sleep cycles and types of dreams. They decided to do some experiments on falling asleep and kept dream journals. Their product was an oral presentation to other students and parents.

The project model gives students control over what to study, how to study it, the time frame for project completion, and the method for demonstrating their learning. But projects do not just happen spontaneously: The model also provides clear rules and planning tools.

To initiate a project, the student must complete a Project Proposal Form. On the proposal, the student outlines a detailed plan, which specifies at least three basic questions that the student wants to answer by doing the project; at least two ways the project is important to the community or world; a schedule of tasks and activities that the student will complete; and three or more resources the student will use, at least one of which must be a person. Another important part of the proposal is an explanation of the state standards that the student will master in doing the project. All students at Minnesota New Country School are familiar with the state curriculum standards, called the Profile of Learning. They know that to graduate, they must eventually meet all of the standards through their projects.

A team that includes the student's advisor and two other staff members must approve each project proposal. Students negotiate with this team the time frame for completion and the number of credits the project may earn (as determined by the time spent on the project, the quality of the work, and the number of state standards mastered). Each student must complete an average of 10 project credits each year in grades 7–12, for a total of 60 project credits to graduate. Each project credit represents about 100 hours of work.

As students work on projects, they maintain a daily record of their activities and progress. At the end of the project, they use a performance rubric to evaluate their success in mastering skills. A team that includes their advisor and other adults also assesses their project for standards met and for lifelong learning skills enhanced.

Each student in EdVisions schools has a personal learning plan that includes personal growth areas and academic needs, which are determined through student assessments. A personal learning plan consists of student data, personal interests, strengths and weaknesses, credits earned to date, attendance records, state standards yet to be met, a plan for the next five weeks, learning style assessment, their scores on the Measure of Academic Progress, levels of engagement, life skill assessments, and project credits earned and in progress. Subcomponents include a personal reading plan and a postsecondary plan.

Many students come to EdVisions schools needing remedial instruction in reading, writing, math, research methods, or other areas. These students receive instruction from school staff to meet their needs. Because advisors are not tied to classrooms and lesson plans, they are available to help individuals or small groups who need remedial instruction. The advisors also offer minicourses reflecting special interests or needs connected with student projects. For example, when several students were working on projects that required spreadsheets, one advisor offered a minicourse on Excel. This structure enables education to be learner driven, customized, contextual, just in time, and collaborative.

Connecting with Students

EdVisions schools are organized around full-time, multi-age advisories. At the Minnesota New Country School, each advisor is responsible for the projects and personal learning plans of 17-20 students. Advisors use an online project management system to track student project proposals, reflections, documentation of time and learning, and student assessments (state standards met, project credits earned, life skills, and so on).

But advisories do more than just promote projects. They are also central to forming connections among adults and students. The advisories meet twice daily to attend to personal and community needs. They create personalized, caring communities. Through the circle process, peer mediation, and restorative justice practices, students and advisors build mutual respect and reciprocity.

To illustrate, consider this incident at Avalon Middle School. One morning, a cell phone and car keys disappeared from a teacher's purse. As soon as the other staff members were made aware of the situation, the teachers called a large circle and discussed the situation with the students. Regardless of what other learning experiences were designed for the day, the incident needed attention. The teacher whose items were missing talked of her need to have the car keys to pick up her children after school. The other teachers said that if the items were returned to a spot outside their offices, no one would be in trouble. Other students talked of how this incident placed mistrust on all of them and how they were hurt that a fellow student would do this.

By the end of the day the items were returned, and the staff and students were relieved. Restorative justice was used to encourage students to think of others and not only of themselves. The incident taught all students that relationships and community are more important than course material.

Ensuring That Students Achieve Intended Results

Project-based schools demand a different kind of accountability. Because the intent is to transform young people into responsible adults, traditional forms of academic assessment do not take center stage. Students never receive a failing grade; if their project team judges that a project is not good enough, the student takes more time to improve it.

Student projects are scored not only on student mastery of state standards, but also on life skills, such as creativity, problem solving, decision making, time management, information gathering, responsibility, and service. These so-called "soft" skills are important ingredients in the personal learning plans and parent-student-advisor conferences. EdVisions schools make it clear that these attributes are just as important as meeting state curriculum standards.

Engaging all Stakeholders

The fourth major component of the EdVisions model is autonomous school management by the staff. Teachers have oversight over budget and staffing, with individual and group accountability for school finance and student success. They engage in self- evaluation and 360-degree evaluation, develop professional learning plans, receive performance pay, and do not have tenure.

The staff at Minnesota New Country School engages in what we call the five Cs:

- Maintaining the collective focus of the school.
- Continually engaging in decision-making using consensus.
- Using coaching and mentoring.
- Using consultation in sharing knowledge with one another.
- Creating community to provide support and learning opportunities.

Teachers model lifelong learning, setting the tone for a community of learners that emphasizes student ownership of their studies and lives. When the adults are in charge of their environment, the students feel in charge of their own environment. This level of autonomy is empowering for both adults and students.

Positive Student Outcomes

Although standardized testing is not the driving force behind the project-based system, it is used for diagnostic purposes and for state accountability. Many educators doubt that students who have control over their own learning can achieve strong results in traditional methods of assessment. Not true. In the past six years, average ACT and SAT scores at EdVisions schools have consistently surpassed national averages.

In addition, evaluation projects carried on in the past few years have found positive results in other areas. Here are two examples.

The Hope Study, conducted by EdVisions, used a variety of student self-perception surveys to assess students' levels of engagement and dispositional hope. The Hope Scale Index, developed by Rick Snyder (2002) at the University of Kansas, is used to determine psychological adjustment. It measures the extent to which an individual is motivated to develop workable goals and to find pathways to accomplish these goals. For example, the Hope Survey includes such statements as, "There are lots of ways around any problem," and "I energetica ly pursue my goals." Each student scores these statements on a Likert scale of 1-8, from "definitely false" to "definitely true."

Hope Scale scores correlate positively with measures of optimism, problem-solving ability, and self-esteem. In addition, studies show that individuals with high hope levels have higher grade point averages, graduate from college at higher rates, and are more successful after college (EdVisions Schools, 2005).

The Hope Study showed that the levels of engagement of students in Minnesota New Country School and similar schools tended to rise as the students progressed through school. Consequently, their hope levels also rose. The study of more than 1,000 students showed that during their six years of schooling, typical students in EdVisions schools raised their hope levels from an average of 47.69 to 53.19. (The national mean is 48.) The study also showed that in traditional schools, engagement tends to stay static or even go down as adolescents move through the grades (Newell & Van Ryzin, in press).

A second study, conducted by a graduate student at Minnesota State University-Mankato (Bezon & Wurdinger, 2008), surveyed Minnesota New Country School alumni and found that 96 percent of graduates had enrolled in two- or four-year programs after graduation, and 69 percent had graduated from two- or four-year programs, with 22 percent still enrolled. Only 9 percent had dropped out of postsecondary education or had not enrolled. When asked about their performance after high school, 91 percent of alumni said their academic performance was good or exce lent. Also rated highly (good or exce lent) by alumni were their levels of preparation in the following skills: creativity, 100 percent; problem solving, 95 percent; decision making, 91 percent; time management, 87 percent; finding information, 100 percent; learning to learn, 91 percent; responsibility, 92 percent; self-directed, 92 percent; leadership, 84 percent; and social skills, 79 percent.

Alumni also rated their reading, verbal, and listening skills highly. Although they rated their formal writing and math preparation less highly overa l, these areas do not appear to have affected them negatively: 92 percent said they believed they were better prepared for college than their peers, and 83 percent said they were better prepared for careers than their peers.

A Promising Model

These studies provide more evidence that the project-based model can create lifelong learners. In 2006, the U.S. Department of Education named Minnesota New Country School one of the eight charter schools in the nation (cu led from 400 nominees) that closed the achievement gap by trying out innovative new strategies (WestEd, 2006). By creating an environment that makes learning the constant and time the variable, uses real-world experiences as learning events, and puts a premium on student maturation and development, the EdVisions model encourages young people to develop into active thinkers who take charge of their own learning.

References

Bezon, J., & Wurdinger, S. (2008). A different type of success: Teaching important life skills through project-based learning. Unpublished document.

EdVisions Schools. (2005). Less, more, and better: A five-year evaluation report from EdVisions Schools. Henderson, MN: Author.

Newell, R..J., & Van Ryzin, M. J. (in press). Assessing what really matters in schools: Building hope for the future. Lanham, MD: Rowman & Littlefield Education.

Snyder, C. R. (2002). Hope theory: Rainbows in the mind. Psychological Inquiry, 13, 249-275.

WestEd. (2006). Charter high schools closing the achievement gap: Innovations in education. Washington, DC: U.S. Department of Education, Office of Innovation and Improvement. Available: www.ed.gov/admins/comm/choice/charterhs/report.pdf

Editor's Note: More information about the EdVisions model, including the 30-minute student-created video on project-based learning, The Mummified Chicken, Mutant Frogs, and Rockets to the Moon, is available at the EdVisions Web site, www.edvisionsschools.org.

Ronald J. Newell is Learning Program and Evaluation Director for EdVisions Schools, Henderson, Minnesota; ron@edvisionsschools.org. Walter Enloe is Professor of Human Studies and Educational Leadership, Hamline University, St. Paul, Minnesota; wenloe@hamline.edu. With Doug Thomas, they are the editors of "The Coolest School in America": How Small Learning Communities are Changing Everything (ScarecrowEducation, 2005).

Chapter 13

Charter Schools: MN 150

The following text was included in the website and brochure containing all the topics nominated for the MN150 exhibit at the Minnesota History Center

Charter schools give parents, teachers, and others the chance to design a school to meet students' needs, without direct control of local school districts. Each of these new schools is granted a "charter" that defines goals and sets limits on how the school is run. Like any public school, a charter school must be open to all, is publicly funded, and involves no discrimination, no tuition, and no teaching of religion. Minnesota is the nation's leader in charter school education. That's the big picture. But the real impact of the national movement that started in Minnesota is best seen up close, by looking at how a charter school can change a student's life. David Kraft had tried, with little success; to thrive at a number of Twin Cities public and private schools before he discovered St. Paul's Avalon School, sponsored by Hamline University. David struggles with the effects of Asperger's syndrome, an autism spectrum disorder that makes it difficult for him to stay organized and focused on meaningful work. He was the classic smart kid who couldn't succeed in a mainstream educational environment. Avalon follows a college-preparation curriculum, with individualized learning plans and project-based lessons. Not only did David complete his high school requirements at Avalon, but in his senior year, he was a key member of the school's State

Academic Decathlon team. A self- described "eclectic geek," David, along with his teammates, took the state championship in the small-school category (less than 650 students). With 120 students, Avalon was the only charter school that participated in the competition. "Avalon really gives us the liberty to do what we want and the responsibility to follow through on our education," said David's teammate Eowyn Ward. Today, there are 1,000,000 students enrolled in 3,700 charter schools in 40 states and the District of Columbia. And within those schools are countless students, like David Kraft, who have found their way to 'academic success.

Used with permission from the Minnesota Historical Society. http://discovery.mnhs.org/MN150

Chapter 14

How a Teacher Partnership Handles a Public High School

Transcript from a discussion of Avalon as a teacher-run school hosted by the Dorsey & Whitney law firm in Minneapolis

When the discussion began about the 'partnership' model in public education there were no partnerships to look at. Today there are. And the interest in this model has risen significantly this past year, with the growing sense that 'better teaching' and 'better teachers' is fast replacing 'accountability' as the key to improving learning.

The effort to "get better people for the job" probably requires that teaching become at the same time "a better job for its people". The partnership model opens into a true professional career for teachers. It works. But many people still have not heard of it. And many who have regard it as a bumblebee; just know it cannot possibly fly.

So we wanted to explore with one teacher-run school -- Avalon School, in Saint Paul -- how that partnership handles professional and administrative matters. Gary Johnson in Dorsey & Whitney had offered to host a discussion, with partners in similar professional fields and people in public education.

"On the witness stand" was Carrie Bakken, one of the founding teachers in this eight-year-old school (www.avalonschool.org). Around the table, to explore these questions, were: Johnson and Peter Hendrixson who'd for six years been managing partner of that Minneapolis law firm; Dan Mott, a partner with Frederickson & Byron, who helped organize the first teacher partnership at New Country School about 1992; Dr. Thomas Marr, medical director for clinical relations at HealthPartners; Richard Bend, an attorney and a founding board member of the Michael Frome Academy, a chartered school which will open September 2008 in Woodbury and will use the partnership model; Beth Hawkins, a journalist commissioned by EducationNext to do an article on teacher partnerships; Jim Miller, a longtime partner with Larson/Allen, an auditing, accounting and consulting firm; Ed Dirkswager, who formerly ran the administrative side of Group Health, was for a time chair of the National Cooperative Bank, and who was later a consultant with Dr. Marr in forming physician practices; Dick McFarland, formerly CEO of RBC Dain Rauscher and ("not today") a board member of the McKnight Foundation; Louise Sundin, past president of the Minneapolis Federation of Teachers; John Maas, at various times a principal, deputy commissioner of the state agency, executive director of the superintendents association, consultant to the school boards association and business manager of a district, in Minnesota K-12; and Jon Schroeder, Tim McDonald and Ted Kolderie of Education|Evolving.

The discussion went about as follows:

Bakken: I'd gone to law school; was going to work with young people in the criminal justice system. But after I taught for a while at PYC, an alternative school in north Minneapolis, I decided I'd rather work with kids in another way. Avalon opened eight years ago. We were sponsored by Hamline University; affiliated with EdVisions. We started with the project-based learning model used at New Country School. We are a cooperative; with no director or principal. We began with eight teachers ('advisers'). We now have 23 people: 16 licensed teachers, five assistants, and two persons in the office. We have grades 7 to 12, but only 36 students in the lower two grades. The summer before school opened we split up all the administrative work. The science teacher knew Quicken so he volunteered to be business manager. I think back: We were so naive at the start; it has been such a work-in-progress. With experience we found it was too much to teach and handle these duties. So we split off separate positions for business manager and program-coordinator. The business manager now does that full-time; loves it; is going for an MBA. The latter position has been shared this year between me and Gretchen (Sage-Martinson). But we're clear: These are not 'authority' positions. Decision-making rests with the group. We all meet weekly. The school is a non-profit with a teacher-majority board: four teachers, two parents, one from the community. We were concerned when one of our founding members, formerly head of the Quaker school here, retired. But we have found the strength is in the group. It is impressive to watch the stability over the years. The coming and going of people does not change the school. Next year I will be back full-time; half-time as program coordinator and half-time as an adviser (teacher).

Personnel

Bakken: We are careful about recruiting, careful to evaluate performance along the way. We try hard to be sure that a teacher coming to the school wants also to be a member of the cooperative; participate in the governance of the school. We don't ask the assistants to take on extra work but we do ask them to take part in the decision-making. We evaluate ourselves. We have had to terminate people. We have to be diligent about professional performance.

Bend: How do you tell whether a new person will be a good co-op member?

Bakken: Usually a diverse background, multiple interests, is a good indicator. We have one teacher who'd spent a career at 3M; another who'd been in the Peace Corps.

TK: Is there an economic dimension to membership? Does a teacher make an investment?

Bakken: No.

Mott: Will Avalon hire if a teacher does not want to be a co-op member?

Bakken: We want all to be members.

Mott: This has been an issue in law firms: Should all be partners, or some simply salaried lawyers?

Johnson: Project-based?

Bakken: The students take a few traditional classes, seminars. Most of their work is on individual projects where they can work at their own pace. So you work with students individually. This means you're not just standing in front of a class all day. If an administrative question comes along you can deal with it at your desk. You can multi-task.

Compensation

Bakken: We try to fo low the Saint Paul salary schedule. We do pay for prior teaching experience. We pay some stipends for extra work. For example, I get something more for the program-coordinator role since I work over the summer. We are very efficient; financially healthy. We carry a sizeable fund balance. We have no director's/principal's salary to pay. A year ago we distributed a 'longevity bonus' and I believe we will again this year. We are still an affiliate member of EdVisions but we are no longer in their payroll/benefits program. Our relationship with them was really helpful, though.

Marr: How does the group handle conflicts over what to do?

Bakken: It's been surprisingly easy. When we know there's a contentious issue coming up we talk a lot ahead. In the meeting we use a "fist of five" system. People hold up five, four, three fingers to indicate some degree of agreement. One or two is disagreement. A closed fist blocks action. We talk it out. It is a group decision. I had been on the personnel committee for some years but I took myself off when I realized that in my role as program coordinator some of the new people were seeing me as a boss. We had an 'administrative team', but gradua ly learned to do without that. You have to work at maintaining this culture. There's a huge learning curve for new people.

Miller: What's the turnover?

Bakken: Low. Last summer we had two leave, to teach abroad.

Miller: To me, this is a sign of success.

Hendrixson: How else do you define success?

Bakken: Our sponsor sets goals; checks to see if we've made them. We have to meet all the state requirements. We're measured. We also do satisfaction surveys.

Hendrixson: What's your feeling about the testing?

Bakken: I wish there were less of it. The Profile of Learning was better for us; more outcome-based. The new standards are very fact-based and specific. There is just a lot of testing. Most of April is lost to testing.

Schroeder: Talk about the students' role.

Bakken: A nice thing about our cooperative is that it models democracy for the students. They wrote a school constitution, the first year. It was a great learning experience for them. And they see their voice matters. Congress meets weekly; any student can join in. How many come depends on the issue. When students are more frustrated, more participate. Initia ly the kids were angry about the dress code; said it was too much like a big district. Congress wrote the dress code. Congress can send us a Bill: The advisers are the 'executive branch'; can veto.

Sundin: How do you evaluate teachers?

Bakken: Initially, with a rubric. Now we use a survey monkey. Every staff member participates. A team reviews. Parents and students are asked, as well. It's anonymous. The key question is whether an adviser is meeting the job-description. What does that adviser do we l; not do well? It ends by asking whether this person should return next year.

Sundin: So you don't use professional standards? Those in state law, or those from the National Board. Some districts develop their own.

Schroeder: Is the nature of the evaluation affected perhaps by the project-based character of the learning program? Do the standards assume traditional teaching?

Bakken: Avalon's job description is very detailed; probably covers all that.

Sundin: Let's discuss this some time.

Marr: How large a school do you think this model would work in? And: Are you subject to more or to fewer state restrictions?

Bakken: It depends. The American History requirements are pretty restrictive. The standards emphasize breadth not depth. But generally we have tremendous freedom. If something is not working we can quickly reverse course. We have now decided to go to classes for math. We decide these things.

TK: Isn't this a function of the autonomy provided to a chartered school, rather than of the partnership model?

Bakken: It's still better when the teachers rather than an administrator decide it. The teachers are better informed. As to scale, I think this model would work in a larger school. At Avalon we have decided not to expand further. But it would work with a larger school. We could figure it out. When we had eight people I could never imagine 23. We think we've shown that at this size a teacher group clearly is capable of making decisions. I think districts could do a lot more site-management on this model.

Student Behavior

Bakken: We have some issues. These are handled by the adviser, not by me. Perhaps with the parents. Sometimes we use mediation.

McFarland: What's the graduation rate?

Bakken: Really high. This year one senior did not graduate.

McFarland: College?

Bakken: At least 85 per cent.

Bend: In what ways have arrangements changed over the years?

Bakken: I mentioned the decision after three years to separate out the business manager and program coordinator functions.

TK: I know your school is legally a nonprofit corporation. Are the teachers formally organized as a cooperative?

Bakken: No.

TK: You're a 'virtual' cooperative, then. The teachers control the board of the school; you delegate to yourselves.

Mott: Avalon is a school in which management is delegated to the employees. They're not a separate enterprise contracted to the school, which was the original idea.

TK: Like New Country.

Mott: Yes.

Bakken: Good point. Currently we're having to set up payroll. Our people had been employees of EdVisions, which handled payroll, etc. Now we've gone to Wells Fargo for this service, and for benefits. So the school is now the employer. We're still sorting this out.

TK: Clearly lots of different things are being tried, with this partnership model. Louise, would you talk about the MFT's idea for 'self-governed schools'?

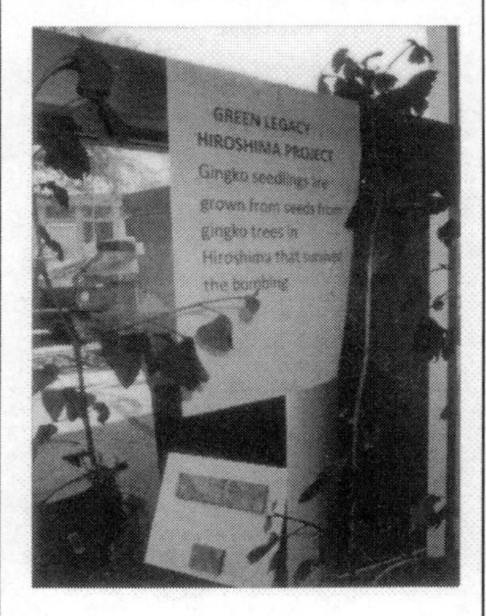

Sundin: Just yesterday we filed the application for a grant for this. In 2005 we'd asked the Legislature for an amendment to the site-management law, to create schools that would be within the district but possibly (my preference) without an administrator; separate enough to have real autonomy. It was strange bedfellows: the MFT and the Business Partnership. Everybody opposed it; the whole 'cartel', as Senator Pogemi ler likes to say. The principals opposed it; still hate it. Even our state union opposed it. But it passed. Implementation has been slow because of all the changes in Minneapolis district leadership. But we have asked about eight groups of teachers if they want to start their own school. In some ways this is like Southeast Alternatives, years ago. There will be a lot of opposition. But there is a lot of discussion about this now, nationally. In the Teachers Union Reform Network, for example. The universal complaint among teachers now is about lousy leadership at the school level. The changing demographics fit into this. It used to be that people came into teaching wanting the security of civil service; a career. We're now getting a younger generation with a different mindset. They want to make a difference; perhaps stay only a few years. And what Ted said earlier is right on: Much of the talk today is about getting "better people for the job"; not about getting "a better job for the people". It's very top-down today; centralized. And this is not working.

Bakken: This past year we've been getting fantastic applications from people who want to come to Avalon; teachers now in districts, who want the sense of ownership.

Sundin: A lot of the best are leaving.

Johnson: There is a question in all kinds of organizations about getting decisions close to the working level.

McFarland: Sure. Our company had maybe 150 branches. Where we had a good branch office we had a good branch manager. Most came up through the company; were basically selected by the brokers in the office. We watch turnover carefully, as an indicator of success. If things aren't working you have to fire somebody.

Bend: It's turning out that the personal characteristics are less important to organizational success than the flow of information, the decentralization of responsibilities. The key is to get the structure right.

Marr: Within any structure there are critical human factors, cultural factors, that shape success. There's no single model that guarantees it.

TK: Is your 'program coordinator' position essentially the 'managing partner' position?

Bakken: I suppose so.

TK: Do you and Gretchen each take half the job, or do you divide the responsibilities?

Bakken: She takes more of the student and marketing questions. I do more in handling the process; compliance, etc.

Q: Could you be fired?

Bakken: That'd be easy. One question on the survey is: Does this person seem confident about the position he or she is in?

Sundin: Another big problem today is the attitude that age and experience are a negative for teachers.

McFarland: Is this because the older teachers aren't keeping up with the technology?

Sundin: No.

Bakken: Experience is important.

Dirkswager: There's no one model for a teacher partnership. The partners can do the administrative work themselves, or delegate it to someone they hire. Lots of possible variations.

TK: We've talked so far about starting with the delegation of responsibility to the school; and about teachers then assuming that responsibility. I want to ask Tom Marr about HealthPartners. Some years back, when it was Group Health, we had a meeting where Dr. Brat explained there were both a corporate board and a medical-dental board. Pretty quickly the teachers were saying: Our district has a corporate board: Where's our professional board?

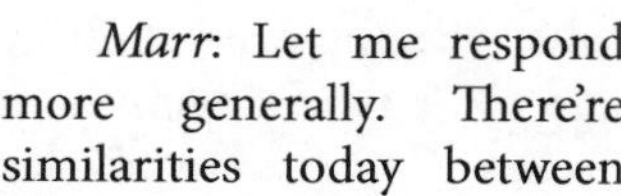

Marr: Let me respond more generally. There're similarities today between health and education. People are dissatisfied. Cost is excessive. Trust in the professionals is slipping. Health care is shifting from autonomy to accountability. In today's world it's the kiss of death to say to doctors, "You just practice medicine". It's a huge cultural change. A structural change, too, driven by the cost of technology and by the growing complexity of managing the business. Successful small groups are se ling their business to hospitals and becoming contracted professional organizations. This is a model in-between the old private practice and the pure employee model. There are some things the business side is accountable for; some things the physicians are accountable for; some things they're accountable for together. Group Health was an employee model; people on salary. In HealthPartners today payment is mostly by productivity. We have about 650 physicians, at 22 practice sites.

Q: What about the Mayo Clinic?

Marr: It is a physician group; a salary model -- now also facing pressures for productivity.

Bend: How do you measure success: by financial results? By patient outcomes?

Marr: It's mostly based on measures of what the physician does: number of patients seen, etc. We also measure satisfaction.

Bakken: I think our model of school is very efficient; financially sound.

Marr: That's why I asked about size.

TK: All the pressures about cost and performance and satisfaction come together to be handled in this teacher-group. We think the national policy discussion about education needs to think much more, now, about the "better job for the people" -- not just in the teachers' interest but in the interest of getting a model that works for the country. Minnesota, again, can be a leader; showing what's developed here. It is a problem that the partnership does not appear in the research. Last year I came across Who Controls Teachers' Work? The author says: teachers don't. I got in touch; asked if he knew there are now schools where teachers do. He didn't; was interested. So we are planning a national meeting this fall to raise the visibility and the priority for this model. Louise has heard this idea discussed at TURN. There's been a session at the national office of the American Federation of Teachers. It might be possible to reach the new president of the NEA. But it will be important to have the help of people who are able and willing to 'testify' to the effectiveness of the partnership model in these other professional fields.

Miller: My people say Minnesota's charter program is good because it provides for 'at will' employees; it is possible to do something when people don't work out.

Sundin: I would note some disagreement with the blanket nature of that. TK: What we've heard re: Avalon is not about the ability of managers to fire employees. It's about the ability and the willingness of the teacher-group to deal with questions of quality and performance when the teachers, rather than an administrator, are in charge of the school. Bakken: It costs way too much to recruit and to train people. We try to help people succeed.

Johnson: We've learned here, too, that it's not an answer just to be able to fire someone. When you're a group you want people to succeed. So you do more mentoring. Dismissal is a last resort; a failure.

Chapter 15

Anti-Bullying Efforts Should Build Trust Between Students and Teachers

Anti-Bullying Efforts Should Build Trust Between Students and Teachers. This editorial was printed in the St. Paul Pioneer Press on March 5, 2012

The author, Brett Campbell, is a Macalester College student and Citizens League member. He is a graduate of Avalon School and has been active in education projects with the Citizens League since 2007. A version of this article also appears in the Citizens League's publication Minnesota Journal.

Attorney General Lori Swanson has been drafting tougher anti-bullying legislation in response to Minnesota's increased bullying problem across countless school districts. According to a Pioneer Press article, Swanson's legislation would require that districts "adopt policies by Jan. 1, 2013, that would prohibit students from bullying or retaliating against victims or those who report bullying and would also establish procedures for immediate reporting, investigation, discipline and potential police notification."

The Pioneer Press quoted Swanson as saying that Minnesota currently has some of the weakest bullying laws in the nation, so it is appropriate that she is looking for a fix.

As a member of the Citizens League's Students Speak Out network, I participated in a working group made up of youths from Minneapolis Public Schools who were charged with addressing school safety. Our findings concluded that increasing trust between students and teachers will reduce bullying and harassment in schools. Our group recognized that bullying is an unavoidable reality, but that there are ways to reduce the number of incidents.

Increasing the exchange of information between students and teachers is the key, but it is crucial that a trusting relationship be established first. This is a cultural problem in our schools that cannot be solved by mandating an informational exchange without addressing how to build the relationship to do so.

Swanson has been quoted as saying that bullying is a result of a cultural problem in our schools, and one that is not entirely preventable. She has that part right. She also has it right that if students are going to report incidents of bullying so adults can help address it, they need to know what adults will do with the information. But her proposal doesn't get to the root of the problem.

Students already know they are prohibited from bullying and that they are expected to report it. They don't share information because a trusting relationship with an adult has not been established first. Simply put, if anti-bullying legislation is to be successful, it needs to address how adults in the school can build these relationships with students.

The Anoka-Hennepin example

How would Swanson's proposed legislation have prevented bullying and increased reporting in the Anoka-Hennepin School District, where recent suicides have made national news and embarrassed Minnesota?

There have been eight student suicides in the past two years, with four said to be directly tied to anti-gay culture in the schools. Nationwide, countless suicides have also been connected to bullying of lesbian, gay, bisexual and transgender students.

Anoka-Hennepin's former policy concerning LGBT issues — which was replaced this month — was known as the district's "neutrality" policy. This policy essentially prevented schools from effectively combating bullying, because it required teachers to stay neutral on matters of sexual orientation. Some Anoka-Hennepin district LGBT advocates said teachers essentially had been placed under a "gag" order concerning the bullying of LGBT students.

If we are serious about preventing the unfair and unwarranted harassment of our students we cannot neglect any harassment.

Culture of accountability needed

Creating a culture of accountability, where students are comfortable reporting harassment, requires all students — LGBT, minority, liberal and conservative — to feel like members of their community. Schools must entertain a positive, nurturing environment to create a culture of safety and accountability.

Schools cannot be afraid to stand up for those who are victimized because of personal politics or religious agendas. Swanson's legislation must take a stronger stance on addressing the trust between students and teachers.

Indeed, if anti-bullying legislation is to be successful, its authors need to turn to schools where trusting relationships and positive environments already exist.

The Avalon example

Avalon School in St. Paul, where I attended eighth grade through graduation, appreciates the validity of a strong nurturing community for the overall benefit of its students. This is not only outlined in the school's mission statement, but also enforced by both teachers and students.

Avalon builds a foundation of trust first, stressing the relationship between teachers and students. Our state needs more schools like Avalon, places where not just some students, but all students are part of a safe community. Swanson's proposal would greatly benefit from taking a closer look at schools such as Avalon and projects such as Students Speak Out.

Swanson is serious about tackling the bullying problem, and so are students. It is about time, and taking on school bullying should be an effort that includes everyone at the table. Our schools are not the place for political battles, and bullying isn't about politics. All people involved in the bullying problem need to work together to define and develop solutions if any new bullying policy is to be successful. This is a fight worth doing right.

Chapter 16

Starting Over

David Pugh has 20 years' experience as a high school math teacher. Here he describes the effects of visiting Avalon on his metamorphosis as a teacher.

For almost 150 years, the education pendulum has been swinging between traditional and progressive approaches (Tyack, 2003). While these opposing views are complex, one way to distinguish them is to picture the final product. In the traditional camp the goal is to fill a child with information and train the student in skills. Progressive educators, however, strive to fill a child with questions and train the student in techniques of inquiry. This dichotomy is referenced by Lynn Olson (1999), describing the impact of Francis Parker on the schools of Quincy, MA (p. 32).

At a time when public schools were dominated by recitation, memorization, and drill, Parker advocated placing the child at the center of education and building schools around their students' motivation and interests . . . textbooks gave way to magazines, newspapers, and materials developed by teachers . . . they studied an integrated curriculum that stressed learning by doing.

That same battle is being fought in my mind and spirit. Five years ago, I entered an EdD program at Hamline thinking I was a master teacher – just adding a "Dr." to my title so I could show others what I great master teacher I was. I could dispense information in a clear fashion and build skills in the clumsiest of students. I had developed effective techniques to prepare students for a standardized test – an essential skill in today's schools. Like the emperor looking in the mirror, however, my experiences in the last five years have shown me the transparency of these techniques for developing a deep, practical, and lifelong understanding of math. I now look at myself as a novice, eager to nurture curiosity and guide students in the art of inquiry. The transformation from master to novice has been the most challenging educational experience of my life.

The Formation of a "Master" Teacher

My own educational experience formed my teaching. Throughout my schooling I strove to do well on tests and bristled at anything that was aimed at a deeper level. I was a master at the school game. From high school to college math and education courses to post-graduate studies in theology, I can't remember ever doing an assignment for any reason except a grade and a credit. Teachers loved me because I did exactly what they asked and I challenged neither their authority nor their methods. I loved school because it consistently rewarded my finely tuned art of regurgitation. I loved school so much I became a teacher.

In 1986 I was trained in OBE (Outcome Based Education), and it fit my style well. My interpretation of OBE was this: Most important is the outcome – the product, not the process. My mantra became "build a good test, and teach to the test," and I became very good at making tests.

Twenty years, two states, three districts, and hundreds of hours of continuing education and curriculum committees only reinforced the teacher-centered one directional transmission of knowledge I had come to know and love as a student. I received grants, won awards, and was often told by students I was the only math teacher they could follow. Many students said my classes were the first math classes in which they felt confident in their abilities. I was cruising smoothly along toward retirement when I began to realize something was terribly wrong.

Mashup: The Perfect Storm & Stand and Deliver

Like the fishing ship Adrea Gail, lost when three fronts came from different directions to form the "perfect storm," I was forced to re-examine my teaching after the events of the 2009-2010 school year. The first wave that hit was the reality that while students were succeeding within the walls of my classroom, their other classes and, more important, their lives remained much the same. Two years earlier I had begun working with fifteen minority students who had failed middle-school math. My goal was to work with them each summer throughout their high school journey in order to give them a better chance at graduating and attending college. These students did well in my classes, but very little of that success transferred to other classes or to life decisions. After two years we still had the expected number of dropouts, pregnancies, and failed classes. I could make math easier, but I wasn't teaching them anything that was applicable outside of my classroom.

The second wave was a woman who began a year-long internship as a student teacher in our math department. She had a background in nursing, engineering, and business, and had a vision for helping students prepare for success in the "real world." Having just voluntarily left an engineering career, she knew what was important – what it would take to make it after graduation. She began asking questions like, "Why do we spend so much time on factoring?" and "Do you really still teach rationalizing the denominator?" What I saw as clever mathematical technique she saw as trivial, even worthless. When she had the opportunity to prepare a lesson, she didn't stand in the front and lecture, but instead created an active exercise. I began to ask myself if what my students were learning had any value in the workplace.

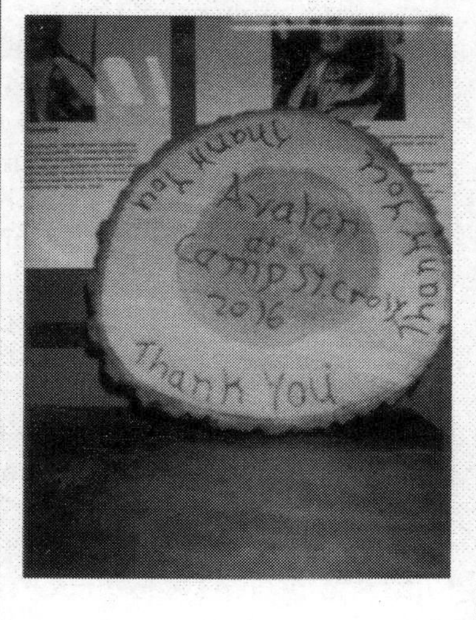

Finally I was hit with the hurricane called "EdD 6", which is a learning community of peers pursuing a Doctorate in Education, led by professors at Hamline University in St. Paul, MN. After one year of coursework, I had listened to NOT ONE lecture, written NOT ONE note, taken NOT ONE test, and bubbled NOT ONE answer sheet, yet I was beginning to transform as a person and as a teacher. I was no longer playing the school game. Thinking for myself and reading for understanding was followed by precise questions and class discussions that kept me thinking for weeks. I wasn't passively spitting back information about teaching; I was becoming a better teacher. These courses were changing who I was, not just what I knew.

Within that storm, my focus in teaching math began to change. No longer could I focus on how fast I prepared students for a test, but instead how wide I could expand their curiosity and how deep I could help them carve out their own understanding of algebra. Gomez-Chacon (2011) calls this "the distinction that should be drawn, in teaching and learning, between attitudes toward mathematics and mathematical attitudes" (p. 147). For years I made math easier for my students, and their attitudes towards mathematics had grown more positive, but had I created mathematical attitudes in my students? Do they approach problems with "flexible thinking, mental openness, critical spirit, and objectivity (Gomez-Chacon, 2011, p. 147), all qualities with enormous value outside the math classroom?" Had I created masters of a few trivial gimmicks used to find x, or had I left in my path novices of the infinite, creative world of mathematics? Were my students becoming experts at the game of school, or beginners at the practice of inquiry? This would change everything.

We're Not in Kansas Anymore

My current teaching practices were based on the model I had seen hundreds of times as a student. I knew there had to be more, and I couldn't be the first person to figure this out. One of my professors, Walter Enloe, suggested I visit Avalon school in St. Paul, so I found some other teachers with similar questions and arranged a visit. From our first step into the building, it was obvious we weren't in a "normal" school.

The most obvious difference was the relaxed yet purposeful atmosphere. That morning I had left my home school building during passing time, or what I refer to as the hallway games. A bell rings and 1,600 students pour into the halls of the building with the singular intent to not make it to their next class during the five minute passing time. Hall monitors stand at strategic spots encouraging students along with shouts of "Keep moving" and "That's not appropriate" and "Take off your hat." It's like a cattle drive. At Avalon, there were no passing times. Students had an agenda and they were responsible to accomplish what they needed. Not every student was on task, just like not every worker in a company is on task at any given time. The difference was this: The students who weren't on task were spending their own time, and in the process of learning time management. It wasn't a game; it was a model of a workplace. Most important, it was humane.

A second difference was the amount of leadership given to the students. I had read about Avalon's democratic environment and their student senate, but this was more than a few gimmicks. There was a sense of pride and responsibility among the students. The atmosphere said, "This is OUR school." In fact, during our three-hour visit we hardly spoke to an adult staff member. Students led our tour, and after that we went to an open area where students were in various levels of study and socialization and initiated conversations about Avalon. When we asked about school rules, one student made it very clear it started with the students. "We're working on the 'pants on the ground' thing, but we (students) haven't come to a consensus yet." I don't think these students were inherently more mature than students at a traditional school, but they were given responsibility and rose to the level of expectations.

The third difference I noted had to do with community. Avalon is a small charter school, so I was expecting a healthy camaraderie among students. Like the island of misfit toys, I expected to find students who, for one reason or another, weren't fitting in to the traditional school environment, and for that common experience to make them more accepting of each other. I believe that is the experience at Avalon, but it goes much deeper. It's not just "I'm OK, you're OK," it's more like "All for one and one for all." I'm sure there are friendship circles within the school, but as hard as we tried, we couldn't find a clique.

When asked about conflicts, one student replied, "Are you kidding? If we get into a fight the restoration process we have to go through takes forever. It's much easier to just work it out ourselves." They were learning to be peacemakers.

New Beginnings

After four years of charter school proposals and school board meetings, I have finally found a place where I can begin a new chapter in my teaching. It's at our districts' alternative school, where I work with a team of teachers helping 9th grade students experience their first success in school. I am thrilled to say I have not given one lecture this year. While I am still a novice, I am finding new ways to introduce my students to math concepts through modeling and self-directed study.

A month ago our principal and several of our teachers took a tour of Avalon, and last week I began my first experience as a project-based teacher with 20 students in one elective class. It is exhilarating yet also frightening after 20 years of teaching to be trying something for the first time. One of my teaching partners commented on how strange it felt for a student to know more about the subject than she, yet we both also found that refreshing.

The highlight of my week was working with a student as he filled out his project proposal. Here's how the conversation went:

"What are you going to do for your project?"
"Cook."
"What are you going to learn about cooking?"
"I already know how to cook."
"So, that's not really learning then, is it? What more do you want to know about cooking?"
"Maybe cooking in another culture."
"OK, so what's the first thing you are going to have to do?"
"Cook."
"Just cook? What are you going to cook?"
"Meat, fish, stuff."
"Do you have a recipe?"
"No."
"So you'll need a recipe."

The conversation went on for fifteen minutes. At the end of our time, this student was well on his way to writing out a list of tasks that he could follow in order to accomplish his goal. From our interaction, I am sure this is the first time he has done anything like that. Over the next four weeks, he will finish his task list and follow that outline to complete a learning experience. The more I reflect on that conversation, the more I believe those fifteen minutes were the most effective fifteen minutes of my teaching career. In those few minutes I didn't transfer information, I helped the student learn what it takes to learn. He can use this in math, but he will also use this in life.

Within the next few years, plans are in place for our school to develop more project-based opportunities for our students. I hope to play a role in helping that happen, and look forward to the day when our students will have more control of their own education. As students individually take more responsibility for learning, I hope we can channel that energy into a democratic student community exercising their rights and responsibilities as citizens of our school. As teachers see students involved in schoolwide decisions, I hope we teachers recognize and respond to our calling of guiding not just our classroom but the overall school climate.

Will we create another Avalon in Rochester? I hope not. Trying to recreate a dynamic, personal, growing, changing organization is not only impossible but counterproductive. Cloning Avalon may sound profitable in the "data-driven", "proven- effective", and "replicate this" session at the latest conference, but Avalon was grown, not manufactured. What we create in Rochester will be what the students and teachers of our school develop as we adapt and adopt Avalon's distinctives of project-based learning, teacher-cooperative leadership, and a democratic learning community. I think we're in for a great ride.

References

Gomez-Chacon, I. (2011). Mathematics attitudes in computerized environments. In L. Bu, & R. Schoen (Eds.), Model- centered learning: Pathways to mathematical understanding using GeoGebra (pp. 145-168). Boston: Sense Publishers.

Olson, L. (April 21, 1999). Tugging at Tradition. Education Week, 18, (32.)

Tyack, D. B. (2003). Seeking common ground: Public schools in a diverse society. Cambridge, Mass: Harvard University Press.

Chapter 17

Taking Ownership of Their Own Learning in Community

Josiah Hill

Almost one year ago I was provided with an opportunity to conduct a study at Avalon School located in St. Paul, Minnesota. I didn't recognize at the time what a powerful and transformational experience my time learning about Avalon and its service to students would be for me and my career as an educator. Up to the time I engaged in this study, I had served as a high school English teacher in a variety of large suburban high schools near the Twin Cities in Minnesota and Philadelphia, Pennsylvania. The schools I have been lucky enough to work within have all been well-regarded and viewed as successful schools that produce high numbers of college bound graduates. These were (and continue to be) great school communities to be a part of and I began to buy into the thinking that all was in place to meet the needs of today's students. To put it mildly, I had become complaisant on many levels. I had developed a high level of confidence that I had been a part of, and continued to be a part of an institution and system that had found the right recipe for serving students in a way that provided them all with a successful pathway forward. I am embarrassed to admit that it had become possible to view the students who failed to benefit from the school's approach as a group of learners who had decided not buy in. In short, it certainly wasn't the fault of the school and the system that was highly regarded that these students didn't succeed or thrive, it was this group's own fault for not taking advantage of what was there. I am humiliated to now recognize that somewhere along the line I stopped clearly seeing these students as the individuals they were and failing to meet them instructionally at their level to meet their individual needs.

Just as I was entering into my opportunity to take a closer look at Avalon, I was noticing an increase in the students I was serving in my traditional school setting failing to fully engage in the work we were doing. It seemed as though it was becoming more regular for students, including some of my most talented students to be holding back and not wanting to take ownership in their own learning. This was manifested in many ways but became incredibly visible when our work would turn toward their senior research papers during their final semester in high school. Students are asked each year to select a topic of their choice and engage in an in-depth study resulting in a 7-10 page paper. It seemed as though large numbers of students were suddenly unable to take the initiative on this process.

Repeatedly as I moved through tried and true exercises that were designed to help students clearly identify interests that could become viable topics, I was met with responses that were unexpected. While some of the more mediocre students appeared to be paralyzed by the scope of the project, it was a new and suddenly common response coming from several of my most gifted writers that startled me the most. Instead of engaging in some introspection to find a path forward that was valuable to them and that could offer an opportunity to pursue learning in an area of passion or interest, many students selected a different route. Suddenly I was met repeatedly with many of my students telling me that they were unable to identify any interests. That they were in need of my direction to tell them what their topic should be and how to proceed. Incredibly concerning was hearing from approximately 10 percent of my students, many of whom who were the most capable, a version of the following statement: "Just tell me what to do and I'll produce it for you." When I refused to do just that and encouraged them to engage in the topic selection exercises designed to provide students with opportunities for self-analysis and self-reflection, many of them struggled to find a topic and a path forward on their own and seemed unable to find traction in the process at hand. Instead of students describing to me an event, a career path, a place, an art form, or a historical figure that they were excited about, I often heard them ask me questions like: "Do you think ______ would be an easy topic to write about?" Others would ask "What topics are other people writing about that I could do too?"

While I had encountered this type of behavior at times in the past, it seemed to have become prevalent almost overnight. In discussion with colleagues, they too discussed their newfound difficulty with getting their students to take the "bull by the horns" on this project and instead now described this process as more like "pulling teeth." I noticed something else that came as no surprise on this project. Because it seemed like fewer and fewer students were tapping into their greatest interests and passions on this project, the quality I had experienced on their work in the past seemed to be more difficult to access. It is no surprise that the work produced by students who chose not to personalize their work by selecting a personally important or interesting topic was lacking in quality. Instead of displaying an interest in growth or learning about a personal passion or a "spark" as I have heard it recently referred to, students instead seemed to increasingly only focus on the acquisition of points to achieve a grade they believe is satisfactory. It didn't seem to be about anything other than them ranking and sorting themselves among their peers rather than developing, learning, and growing.

When I arrived at Avalon to learn more about their approach, one of the first welcoming faces I came in contact with was Kieren. Kieren served as an advisor at Avalon and welcomed me into his classroom and offered to take part in an in-depth interview as a part of my study. He described to me what drew him to Avalon away from a large, highly regarded local suburban high school. He referenced the difficulty experienced by teachers in a system where they were charged with working to connect with and getting to know well over 150 students at any given time. A place where students were more interested in grades than learning. A place where parents were becoming increasingly interested in the pursuit of points and grades rather than the learning itself. It was becoming a place where Kieren indicated that he felt like he was moving down the wrong path and away from educating students in more valuable and effective ways he had envisioned and experienced in the past. "I was worried that maybe, maybe I was done doing teaching the way I had initially conceived of teaching" (Personal Interview, 7/2/2015). These feelings and experiences led him to seek an opportunity to become a teacher-advisor at Avalon.

In a senior project a Avalon School that is similar, but more encompassing than the research project I have experienced at the traditional school where I have most recently taught, Kieren described some of the key differences in how students view and experience their learning. Instead of a quest for points on the way to achieving a certain grade level, Avalon students seem to experience learning on a much deeper and more meaningful level. His description painted a picture that was quite different from what my own students at were experiencing on their own senior research projects.

> Because I think the senior project for some students starts as a school assignment—"Oh this is what I've got to do if I want to participate in graduation at Avalon." And, what happens is, whether they come in as seniors, or when they're younger they see this as being this daunting assignment...What usually ends up happening is this very deep exploration of something that at the very least they are interested in, but most likely it is something that they care very deeply about. Then something happens inside of them. And...almost all of the senior projects are ultimately projects about themselves, and trying to understand who they are as learners, and how do they envision themselves in the world after Avalon...Just through the process many students start to try and think about 'well, how is this going to translate into what I want to do after Avalon.' So what starts off as an assignment or a requirement, by the end when a kid finalizes...that feels like 'I've done something now that was a big deal.' And not that it was a requirement or not that 'now I'm going to graduate.' But more 'I've learned something about myself that maybe I didn't know before." (Kieren Wilson, Interview Response, 7/2/15)

I share this description and this difference as a powerful example of the difference in learning experiences and approaches between what I was a part of with students in the traditional high school where I served and what was taking place at Avalon.

Another staff member I interviewed described this phenomenon in a slightly different way. Advisor Bonnie Young described why she believed the engagement and learning at Avalon rose to levels much greater than her past experiences at more traditional high school settings. Empowering Avalon students to design much of their own learning journey provides a key ingredient in them taking much greater ownership over their work. At one point in the interview she adopted the voice of a traditional school teacher speaking to a traditional school student in an effort to use humor make this point. "You can think about things deeply if you want to, but you don't necessarily have to because we will lay out everything that you need to do. And if you just do these things, you'll pass. Right down to standardized testing." Her comments here reminded me of the experiences I have had working with students in the schools where I have taught including those I mentioned above. In the experience of the staff members I spoke to at Avalon, the act of authentic student empowerment to take part in and ultimately make decisions about their education leads to students taking a great deal of ownership over their own learning.

Avalon graduates too felt it was important to have influence over their own learning during their time there. Feeling empowered to make decisions about how they would engage in mastering the state standards allowed Avalon students to take their learning to a deeper level. Unfortunately, I have been in proximity to many educators during my career that would downplay or even dismiss the importance of student choice in the classroom. Avalon's approach to serving students is based directly on the importance of this concept. This foundation has proven to be a sound one that has enabled a great deal of student success and has fostered a sense of student ownership over their work throughout their time at the school.

> It is the choice that makes all the difference. since you've chosen it, you have a personal investment and ownership of the project, which carries through to the final product, as well as to what you actually learn...If you're doing a project that you care about, that you've designed, and that actually matters (it counts towards completing school), then you gain something when it's done: if it went well, you have a feeling of accomplishment; if it went poorly, you learn about your weaknesses...Avalon's motto is "passion for learning" and it suits Avalon perfectly. (Survey Respondent, 4/14/15)

Another recent graduate added an additional layer to this thinking and expanded on the motivation Avalon's approach fosters and allows to develop in learners there.

> I found that after I switched [transferred] to Avalon, and I realized that school and education wasn't something that I am forced to do to get a good grade on some test that everyone and their mothers' will judge me on, I could really grow as a person. I found that education was true curiosity and that with the desire to know something and the strive to find the answer, I learned things, not just memorized them. (Survey Respondent, 4/20/15)

Instead of simply going through the motions, these recent Avalon graduates describe the impulse to learn and grow based on the conditions present in their learning environments. "It's easier to feel motivated to learn when you are invested and interested in your own education" (Survey Respondent, 4/24/15).

While these descriptions of recent experiences at Avalon were exciting to hear about as an educator, the questions that were (and continue to be) more interesting for me as an educator are: What conditions allow for this kind of learning to take place? What is it that must be present for students to feel compelled and excited to take ownership over their own learning and growth? In order to answer these questions, I think it is important to listen deeply to the words and perspectives shared by both the graduates and staff members of Avalon as they describe the conditions present and surrounding their learning experiences during their time there. Before examining the experiences of stakeholders at Avalon, a short description of the focus on building and sustaining community and the value placed on this concept will help to set the table for what many of them share.

In their 2014 work *Deeper Learning: How Eight Innovative Public schools are Transforming Education in the Twenty-First Century*, authors Monica Martinez and Dennis McGrath described the need for learning in community as essential for deeper learning. Avalon and the other schools described in this text are presented as holding "fast to the belief that developing students into self-directed, responsible learners concerned for the learning of others is a fundamental requirement for Deeper Learning" (p. 25). Martinez and McGrath go on to comment that developing learners into self-directed students who come to take ownership over their learning is and immense challenge and one that requires more than the efforts of a single teacher and instead must include an intentionally and constantly sustained school-wide culture focused on the concept of community.

> What is demonstrated vividly through Avalon... is the power of a learning community to transform students' lives when a culture exists that values relationships, trust, and respect, and simultaneously presses students consistently to do their best—by the setting of high expectations, and the support and encouragement needed to meet them—through a collective responsibility for learning" (p. 25)

One of the conditions clearly present at Avalon that I have not encountered in the traditional schools I have spent time in proximity to is a strong sense of authentic community. While it was clear that there was a different feel to Avalon when I spent time there, it wasn't something that I could put my finger on in my initial tour of the school (before I had an opportunity to interact closely with students and individual staff members). My understanding of the genuine feeling of community present there grew as I heard students, staff members, and graduates describe it, its importance, and its impact on their learning and their lives. As I learned more about the school, it became clear that this powerful characteristic did not develop by mistake. The founders of Avalon made certain that conditions were present to ensure this school had a strong focus on building community both inside and outside of the school walls. While I came to see how the entire school community experiences this strong sense of togetherness and responsibility to the others present, this critical characteristic of Avalon is most readily on display in the individual advisories that make up each class.

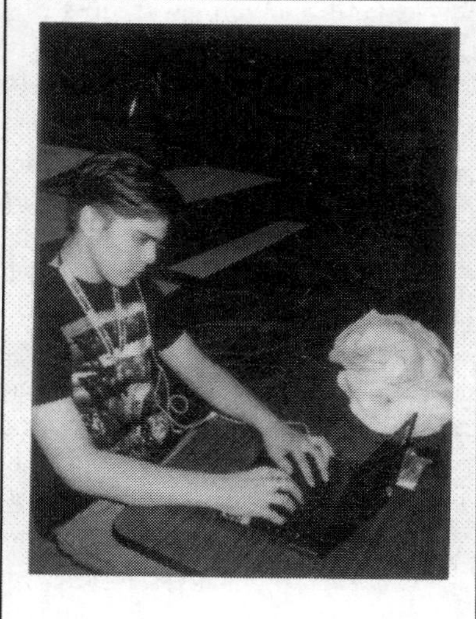

Building a learning community is not something that can be done once and expected to continue into perpetuity. In an interview with teacher/advisor Kieren Wilson described his desire as an Avalon staff member to develop students into individuals who connect and care for those around them—both in school and in their lives outside of school as well. He stated that Avalon wants students to "become people that are engaged in their community because communities get built when people are involved. Like,

Avalon has to rebuild itself every fall. We have to start over. 60 or 80 new students arrive and we have to start over and build it. Our community is only as good as the thoughtful effort that we put into building it" (Kieren Wilson, Interview Response, 7/2/15).

Repeated responses provided by Kieren pointed to the intentional work engaged in at Avalon to ensure that students are able to perceive their role as citizens of the larger community. He made it clear that this dimension of learning would serve student both during and well after their time at Avalon. "If you work with students to try to build a community, they develop critical skills that they need to be successful in the world after Avalon. How to listen to others, how to reach consensus, how to disagree respectfully, how do you maintain your space and communal space. You know, it makes you a good roommate, it makes you a good worker, it probably makes you a good human being." Kieren expressed that this focus on citizenship development was something that was born out of and made possible due to the cooperative structure at Avalon. He also expressed that this kind of sustained focus on social responsibility isn't typically possible within a traditional school structure.

Staff member Bonnie Young believes that the learning community culture of the school leads to students expanding their awareness of those around them as well as an opportunity to learn from others. When I asked her what makes a student an engaged citizen she focused on a definition that was on both a small and large scale. "Knowing what is going on around you…Whether it is what is going on in your little social circle or what is going on out there in the world." In her estimation, this knowledge of what is happening around them leads students to deeper and more engaged learning. "I think it creates engaged learners. I think it creates engaged citizens—just engagement in the world around you. Whether that is on a very micro, or a huge macro, worldly scope."

Several survey respondents also referred to the sense of community as having a major impact on their experience as a student at Avalon and how it continued to impact them following graduation. The sustaining of a nurturing community that included everyone at Avalon allows all students to learn and grow. The importance of this community feel (that many describe as significantly different from other schools these graduates had attended before Avalon) was repeatedly referenced by survey respondents. "The community at Avalon was truly unique and helped me become who I am today" (Survey Respondent, 5/5/15). Not only was this sense of community different at Avalon, it clearly and uniformly impacted learners in a positive way. "The community was very supportive. It was definitely the biggest, key part of my successful learning environment" (Survey Respondent, 5/1/15). Another participant added that this community included a balance of valuing individuality while promoting the health of the entire group. "The support I received from the student community was outstanding. Everyone cared about everyone else's welfare but gave each other space to develop as individuals. No student was overbearing and everyone took charge of their own education" (Survey Respondent, 4/28/15). Clearly during their time at Avalon the approach allowed for all to feel welcomed and supported. "Avalon offers a community of acceptance which makes it difficult for students to fall between the cracks. Students and teachers at Avalon care about one another and encourage each other to succeed" (Survey Respondent, 4/28/15).

Other survey respondents shared thoughts about the lasting impact of experiencing the essence of true community that was present at Avalon. Not only did it support them as learners while at the school it has provided a lasting impact on how some conduct themselves day-to-day as adults. "The community taught me I was loved and supported and had the strength to love and support others and that has drastically affected the way I live my life today. These are definite benefits" (Survey Respondent, 5/15/15). Another graduate survey respondent added to this sentiment stating that Avalon "taught me that I should have a voice not just in my own education but in my community and in the world. In this way, Avalon creates leaders and activists who graduate with strong voices and the means to make them heard. (Survey Respondent, 4/19/15). The Avalon focus on community has clearly stayed with many of its alumni.

Recent graduate Kristof Peterson spoke about the importance of the teacher-advisors' ability to model this sense of community in ways that are not necessarily possible in traditional high school settings. "The fact that they have the co-op model…a more democratic model I guess. It is definitely different in that they [teacher-advisors and other staff members] have a direct say in the direction the school goes in and it is different in [that] the relationships with the students [are] much closer because they are involved" (KP Interview response 7/26/15). He stated that this provided an excellent example to the students of how to conduct themselves as a responsible and self-directed member of the learning community as a whole. Teacher-advisors were able to closely connect with students due to the advisory structure. They were there "making sure you are doing things that are interesting to you as a student. This means they get to know you too. They get to know your interests and your desires and things like that. Because of all of this they seem more invested in the success of the students" (KP Interview response 7/26/15).

The relationships students developed at Avalon were clearly strengthened by this sense of community modeled by the staff there. "I think it happens when you are working closely every single day with people...Having that, it feels like there is more of a community when everyone is right there. You see each other and talk to each other when you are working on things. When you have a sense of ownership of your space in a way too, that creates a sense of community too (KP Interview response 7/26/15)." This sense of community allowed for relationships that not only supported each student's individual learning, but allowed for the development of a community strong enough to tackle difficult topics or work through challenges within the school during its first few years of operation.

Avalon's authentic community was described near the end of the graduation ceremony in June of 2015. One of the school founders Dr. Walter Enloe, who is a local professor at Hamline University's Graduate School of Education, stated it clearly and succinctly when he addressed the graduating seniors and the audience with this description of what sets Avalon apart. Near the end of his address to the graduating seniors, he spoke about the human connections that serve as the most important aspects of the school. "It's the people. It's the relationships. Avalon is a place where you are known." It was clear throughout this ceremony that these connections were at the core of the Avalon experience and the sense of community cultivated there had a profound impact on the graduates and families gathered at the ceremony.

My time spent at Avalon has led me to the strong belief that for students, **Deeper Responsibility Leads to Deeper Learning.** As stated by Martinez and McGrath (2014), "The interplay of student and teacher autonomy is key to building safe, trusting communities and also to creating the kind of open culture necessary for meaningful learning to take place" (p. 44). This section of that text seems to be hinting at what I believe results when the conditions and culture of trust and empowerment for students and teachers are present within a school community. The stakes have to be high for this to be perceived by all as real. Newell and Enloe (2008) describe the valuable symbiotic relationship between student and teacher autonomy present at EdVisions schools. "When the adults are in charge of their environment, the students feel in charge of their own environment. This level of autonomy is empowering for both adults and students." If provided with a quality example of autonomous adults working together and being trusted to do quality work (like students are at Avalon), a school's students will follow suit. It seems as though the students and adults will feed off of each other in an amplifying process that increases learning and growth for all.

The second layer to this is intentionally adding an unyielding focus on strong community and strong respect for others and their learning. One element that is present in, and rings true through the voices of the participants in this study, is the ongoing reinforcement of these focal points through the modeling of Avalon's teacher/advisors. This is evident in their daily interactions where they model learning alongside their students. It is modeled in their handling of shared responsibilities associated with the co-op structure of the school that is void of a hierarchical construct. It is evident in how they work to empower their students to both own their work and to support the other members of their learning community.

When I step back from the intensity I experienced while I engaged in conducting this study and think about how many of the elements of Avalon would fit or play out in the traditional school systems I have experience operating within, I'm excited and troubled at the same time. It is my opinion that the so-called "accountability era" that the realm of public education currently finds itself within either doesn't allow space for, or (on some levels) is directly opposed to these elements becoming mainstream components or experiences for students in our traditional school settings. The pressure to chase blindly after greater success on the almighty standardized exam that has been deemed the most important at any given moment, has increasingly left the most important focal point of education unconsidered: the students themselves. Instead of keeping a focus on the learners, attention has instead amassed surrounding only the tests themselves leading to a single-minded emphasis on

lessons designed to increase test scores at all costs. The greatest cost of all associated with this thinking is the mortgaging of student opportunities to take control of their own learning and their engagement in authentic and meaningful deeper learning. The damage caused by this is immeasurable. Most notably this causes harm to the students and their interests and passion for learning what is meaningful to them. This approach also weighs heavily on the educators themselves as they are forced to increasingly remove their focus from the students they serve and care about due to the pressures placed upon them surrounding test scores. This trend is severely distressing to me and is exactly why I found my time at Avalon to be so invigorating and exciting. It provides a clear example of how things can be different. How students can operate in a learning community that allows for them to pursue learning in their interest areas and surrounding their passions. Learning that they find meaningful enough to take ownership of and pursue in a self-directed manner. To quote Dr. Enloe's address at the 2015 commencement ceremony, "Avalon is truly a place where you are known" and this makes all the difference.

Deeper Learning, Deeper Leading: Avalon School

Chapter 18

Dialogues: Social Construction and Avalon School

Travis A. Erickson

What is Avalon School and the reality is has created? How does it differ from institutions in public education? The first section will tend to the history and present essence of the school, highlighting how it stands apart from other educational institutions. The second section will outline and explore constructionist and relational theories, focusing primarily on how we as social beings co-create meaning and our understanding of the world. While these first two parts take a descriptive approach, the third will be prescriptive, bringing together the constructionist perspective and applying it to the educational practices and community at Avalon. However we might find these theories present within the school, they hold additional implications for organizations, institutions, and relationships outside of a private or charter school setting. It is to this that we will turn in section four. Avalon school (Descriptive)

History and Origins (Diachrony)

Every moment has a history. In the history of language, for example, we might consider how it is that meaning changes over time. In the history of an organization we might recognize how the initial cultural foundations affect the ways in which decisions are made months and years down the line. With this in mind, we can see how an understanding of the present moment is both dependent on and enriched by the recognition of that moment's history.

Avalon School was founded in 2001. It was organized as a charter school in St. Paul, Minnesota. As of this writing it serves over 200 students in grades 6 through 12. There are many descriptions, numbers and other measures that account for the reality that Avalon has created -but before we examine the Avalon of today we should consider the history, conversations, and moments from which Avalon came. While there are several written accounts authored by parties very much involved in the school's conception and formative years, I will provide a brief overview from their narratives.

The founding of the school began in 2000 with a collective of teachers, parents, grant writers and community members from St. Paul, Minnesota and the surrounding area. From the start the purpose appeared simple, this was a group of adults coming together to create an organization that would transit values, create a nurturing environment, and sustain a self-driven learning community. This was a group, that more than anything was bound by the excitement and the possibility of starting something very different within the model of public education.

From the start, however, the founders struggled to agree on the basic principles of the institution -each could voice what they were doing, but their reasons for why were directly at odds. Of the founders, parents had an interest in creating a school where they had a say in determining who worked with students, several saw it as an opportunity for making money or securing employment, and others held to a vision of replicating the model of Minnesota New Country School-a successful charter school that set in motion the practice of project-based learning in the state.

The dynamics of the conflict changed in favor of those supporting the Minnesota New Country School model and a teacher led school after the founders secured grant funding through the Gates Foundation. With this grant came expectations regarding the style of curriculum and leadership at the school-specifically, requirements favoring a model of project-based learning and shared governance.1

Much of the organizational and curricular blueprint was adopted from Minnesota New Country School, but Avalon expanded on the model in ways we'll soon explore. Looking at the first recruitment postcard sent to teachers across the state in 2001 you'll find a compelling proposition spelled across the front: "What if teachers could design the ideal school?" Turning the card over you find a call for the construction of "imaginative, creative and disciplined learning communities."2 This was not a simple call for employees; it was a request for inspired teachers to take ownership for the imagination and realizations of a new institution. It was a call to pull together a community of teachers to jointly construct the ethos of a school. Surprising too is the confidence in the founders' attitudes towards ambiguity, improvisation, and uncertainty in the anxious months before opening day.

What followed this initial call were the first hires -teachers who participated in the defining dialogues that shaped the mission, organization and recruitment efforts for the school. All conversations are negotiations on some level -they are how we as social beings arrive at a shared reality. The initial conversations at Avalon were foundational negotiations in constructing the governance and operational realities of the institution. Out of these conversations came the mission for the school. It is layered but simple-unique in that you can say it with a single breath: "Avalon School prepares students for college and life in a strong, nurturing community that inspires active learning, engaged citizenship, and hope for the future."3 This as much as anything, has been a common thread over the school's 15-year history.

Organizational Structure and Present Essence (Synchrony)

So where do we find the school some fifteen years later and how has it adapted over the years? Though proudly focused still on the values of its founding, the Avalon of today looks and feels different. Different entirely is the building in which the school first occupied. Changing still is the student body, which has expanded in both its size and demographics.

Visiting the school for the first time can be a bit misleading. It doesn't look like what most imagine a school "should look like". Following a side street through an industrial part of St. Paul, between warehouses and loading docks, you find a simple gray and brick building-this is Avalon School. Instead of soccer fields, playgrounds, and tennis courts, there is a place for a small garden and a single wooden picnic table.

Walk through the main doors and you'll notice it is in many ways the same and in other ways wildly different from traditional high schools in the state. Replacing the narrow, locker-padded hallways are open spaces, vaulted ceilings, common areas, and classrooms with windows to both the inside and out. The composition is organic and the student energy and engagement seems very fluid-by design. Outside near the garden and hand-built chicken coop is table with an advisor leading a small book discussion, inside are students scattered about reading, working on computers, paper, and canvas. A few wander the halls, perhaps just for the sake of wandering.

While opening day was host to 120 students in grades 9 and 10. Today the community of students has nearly doubled and expanded to grades 6 through 12. The students that Avalon serves, although from the Twin Cities, are not exactly a representative sample of the surrounding area. Similar to metropolitan schools in the state, one third of students qualify for free or reduced price lunch and nearly the same number (29%) are from minority races.4 However, Avalon attracts those who for a variety of reasons, felt marginalized or struggled in a traditional educational environment. The number of students eligible for special education services is 26%, nearly twice the state average.5

Likely, you wouldn't imagine a school like Avalon to remain in one place for too long. The very nature of its community and curriculum has driven what in hindsight appears to be an organic progression. That said, one element of relative permanence is the teaching staff. You can still find several of the first teachers working at the school some fifteen years since its founding. Additionally, the annual teacher retention rate is above 95%6 -nearly 10 points higher than the rest of Minnesota.7

At present, the 32 full-time staff includes 18 advisors, 10 educational assistants, two social workers, and two administrative staff. All members to this staff have equal voice in the organization. Avalon contracts with private providers to oversee the finances, payroll, federal and state reporting obligations, custodial services and other administrative tasks-freeing up time for the teachers to focus on the students and the learning environment.8

Governance

The school was founded to operate as a teacher cooperative. Six of the 11 seats on the board are filled by teachers, giving them the majority.9 The staff has equal voice in day to day operations, hiring decisions, and other aspects of the organization's operation.

Avalon adopted a familiar, three-branch model of governance. The school's student congress serves as the legislative branch, drafting rules and amending the constitution. The formation of the school's constitution itself is an example of project-based learning and active citizenship.10 The executive branch is composed of the Avalon staff, who not only appoint members to serve on the governing board, but hold power to veto legislation passed by the student congress. The judicial branch of Avalon consists of peer mediation and restorative justice. While the Student Congress addresses school wide dilemmas, peer mediations work to resolve conflicts between individuals. The process is used to resolve student to student, student to staff, and staff to staff conflicts. Explicit in the Avalon Constitution, under the Bill of Rights and Responsibilities, you find every person at the school has the "right to bring someone to mediation" and the "responsibility to attend mediation when asked at a reasonable time."11

Worth noting is that the judicial branch was first conceived as a court system with a panel of judges who earned their credentials by passing an evaluation on the School's Constitution -a Bar Exam of sorts. This panel of judges would hear any and all cases that were not first settled through peer mediation. The requirement of sending cases first to an alternative form of dispute resolution (processes other than litigation) is similar to the judicial systems seen in many state and federal jurisdictions; the aim being to reduce cost to parties, ease overwhelming court dockets, and take a collaborative or transformational approach to resolving disputes. At Avalon it worked so well, that in the first year of operation not a single case made it to court, as they were all settled through mediation. In response to this, the school moved to a system that functioned entirely on peer mediation and restorative justice.

Approaches to Learning

What is it about Avalon that sets it apart from public schools in the area and across the nation? Aside from the teacher cooperative model and shared governance, the school's curriculum is built from a different pedagogical mindset. The ideas central to the mission, present in their commitment to deeper learning, and lived every day by staff and students are to maintain a small learning community, a self-directed project-based learning program, use authentic assessment, and function through teacher-ownership and democratic governance.12

Small Learning Communities: "How do we connect with young people in a democratic learning community?"13 In a small community of learners there is a focus on maintaining a size that allows for positive relationships and promotes an environment of high touch, student-centered learning. Small communities are organized into multi-age classrooms ("advisories" at Avalon), and students have the opportunity to engage with parents and the larger community. Here too we find an emphasis and commitment to learning through service.

Self-Directed Project-Based Learning: "How do we facilitate the work of youth as self-directed producers and learners?"14The primary focus of project-based learning is driven by a constructionist philosophy.15 Projects, both group and individual, are tailed to the needs of students and employ multiple approaches in teaching and learning. There is a recognition of student interest in project-based learning, as well as an emphasis on preparedness for a college environment, the work-place, and active citizenship.

Authentic Assessment: "How do we know that we are achieving our intended results?"16 Efforts aimed at a more authentic form of assessment include: using value-added measures, personalized learning plans, involving the community in public presentation and feedback of student work, and tracking student work through electronic portfolios. Additionally, student projects are assessed by multiple adults within the school.

Teacher-Ownership and Democratic Governance: "How do we engage 'Teachers as Owners' of a democratic learning community?"17 The teachers have control over the budget, hiring, and hold accountability for the school's financial viability and educational achievements. This model is a lived democracy, and extends the ownership in decision making to the teaching staff of the school.

These four pillars were adopted from the Minnesota based non-profit EdVisions, whose work in educational development began with Minnesota New Country School in 1993. It was through the success of this school that EdVisions was able to secure grant funding and expand their model to small schools in Minnesota and Wisconsin. Avalon contracted with the organization and is now member to a network of schools across 10 different states

While Avalon started from and still remains true to the approaches to learning outlined by EdVisions, the institution has grown in new directions since its opening. In the years since its founding, the school has invested in the process of guiding students to a "socially and intellectually responsible adulthood;" working to sustain an environment in which students can cooperatively discover who they are who they want to become.18 It is a process that is democratically negotiated, improvisational at times, but wholly deliberate in its purpose and composition.

Social constructionsim (Descriptive).

To understand the foundations, directions, and intentions of Avalon it may help to first explore the constructionist mindset from which much of the school and community was built. To begin, constructionism is a theory of knowledge. It is most often catalogued under the philosophical umbrella of epistemology; and like other perspectives in epistemology, it is concerned with the nature of truth, the sources of knowledge, and the validity of our beliefs. With a mind towards sharpening this lens onto Avalon school, it is to these theories that we turn.

Social Construction

Where social constructionism sits within the debate is not so much along a spectrum, but in a dimension both intersecting and separate from the earlier theories. Positions in construction are drawn from vantages far removed from innatism and empiricism.

The constructionist is not concerned with individual cognitive process and their role as it relates to knowledge. Instead, social construction finds its primary focus on the reflexive and relational roles in meaning-making, language, and belief systems. Working from this perspective, knowledge, language, and our understanding of the world are born through relationships; knowledge is not -as the empiricists would have it-a "neutral study of an objective truth."19 Rather, our individual realities and our collective assumptions are products of tradition and shared understanding.

Constructionist and relational theories may at first seem at odds with the individualist, Western traditions of accounting for the self and the ways in which we make sense of the world.

Recognize that it is from the individualist orientation that we view the structure of relationships as groupings of separate selves. The self is the building block from which our associations, relationships, and organizations are both built from and reducible to. Positions in social construction hold opposing distinctions of the self. The constructionist sees individuals as products of relationships-suggesting that "what we take to be knowledge of the world grows from relationship, and is embedded not within individual minds but within interpretive or communal traditions." Even an isolated individual thought is composed of images and languages shaped by our social histories-"we are made up of each other."20

When we talk about the relational nature of things we are concerned with their connections. The connection of primary interest here is reflexive-it is one that sustains a cyclical, dialogical momentum of cause and effect. From a constructionist vantage, there is a distinction between a person and a self. Persons are recognized as individual bodies, while selves are constructions of relations. 21 The self is an ever-changing representation of our reflexive relations. It is built from and sustained through relationship.

Not that our individual psychologies should be disregarded, but upon closer inspection we might find our concept of pure individualism suspect. Any thought, while seeming to originate inside the individual is built in response to or in tandem with the social. The psychological, personal self is built from the social-the sense of an individual self is constructed from social interactions, social comparisons, and shared experience. Consider even our most personal beliefs and ideologies; though central to self, we did not arrive at them individually. These webs of associations, attitudes, and emotional charges have origins or intersections with social experience, culture, and interpersonal communication. At the most basic level each element of our realities-from the most concrete to the most abstract-has a social history, and it is through this social history that they acquire meaning. In this sense, the self is inseparable from the social.

Much of what we consider to be knowledge about the world exists in the form of objective facts, institutional facts, and shared beliefs. Objective facts, such as the physical properties of a hydrogen atom, or the distance along Highway 1 from San Francisco to Carmel, California are considered to be empirical and concrete. Institutional facts on the other hand, such as the institution of marriage, the notion of private property, the use of paper money, or the recognition of a county line between Santa Clara and Monterey County, are built to serve social functions. On first consideration, the difference between objective facts and institutional facts appears simple; the former is concrete and pre-determined, while the latter is created through social exchange. We could not, for example, legislate to change or wish away the duration of an hour, Pacific tide cycles, or the density of mercury. However, objective facts and institutional facts have a similar origin. It is an origin embedded in relationship and the co-creation of meaning. These facts, our knowledge, and beliefs can exist only through human agreement -because as humans, we generate meaning together.22 Knowledge, society, and the world itself are made, they are invented, they are socially constructed.

We can bear the weight of these institutional facts, present in most every moment, because we have been raised to recognize their existence as concretely as the brute and "objective" facts around use. "The child is brought up in a culture where he or she simply takes social reality for granted. We learn to perceive and use cars, bathtubs, house, money, restaurants, and schools without reflecting on the special features of their ontology and without being aware that they have a special ontology."23

Relational Responsibility

The self is inseparable from the social. "Thinking, knowing, believing, and self-understanding, all have their origins in social interchange. Mind, in effect, is inseparable from social process."24 If we return our focus to the social aspects of social construction, what might we find in terms of the nature of relationships and our responsibility towards them? If the products we value so much: knowledge, language and truth are born through a process of relationship, what does that suggest about our accountability towards that process? If meaning is co-constructed through relationship, then perhaps we have a relational responsibility. Expanded further, to be responsible to relational processes it to "favor the possibility of intelligibility itself-of possessing selves, values, and the sense of worth."25

Our relationships are not a game of chess, we are not sending letters back and forth; they are more synchronous than an action and reaction, existing both before and between a call and response. Our actions are coordinated. Within every dialogue and in all of our relational exchanges we carry from the past the memory of similar exchanges, we hold in the present the conversation of the moment, and we pull from the future our expectations and anticipations of where this dialogue might lead us. Constructionists call this type of coordination "joint action," and it is explained as a phenomenon that can neither be "carried out alone nor can it be reduced to the mere summation of individual actions."26

Through social construction we find that "any way of identifying or describing the self is also dependent on relationship. Thus, any language purporting to describe the mental world of the individual-the language of perception, memory, emotion, desire and so forth-is a by-product of culturally and historically located traditions. The self-both in terms of public identification and private surmise-is born of relationship."27 Then it is towards this sense of relationship that we should feel deeply accountable, and it is with this in mind that we turn to the constructionist examination of Avalon School.

Social construction at Avalon (Prescriptive)

If we accept the position that knowledge, meaning, and value is born through relationship, it should follow that our lives, schools, and institutions might benefit from encouraging and supporting the relational aspects of all we do. Avalon was intentionally and referentially founded on principles in social construction. Intentional is their approach to a bottom-up production of knowledge through project based learning and the embodiment of "learning through doing". Referential is the school's attention to relationship and reflexive processes in their community and curriculum. Before looking at how social constructionism is enacted at Avalon, let's consider the pedagogical directions and dispositions authored within the perspective.

Constructionist Pedagogical Alternatives

It is not as if perspectives in social construction propose to wholly abandon practices in traditional education. What they do suggest, however, is a greater attention to:

1. Greater democracy in negotiating what counts in educational practice;

2. The local embedding of curricula;
3. The breaking of disciplinary boundaries;
4. Education practice in societal issues;
5. A shift from subject and child-centered modes of education to a focus on relationships.28

Many of these ideas, as we'll explore, are present in the curriculum and learning environments that are created between students and advisors at Avalon. A few of the many practices that employ or embody these ideas include reflexive deliberation, collaborative classrooms, polyvocal pedagogy, and the view of knowledge as participatory.29

Reflexive Deliberation provides a way in which students can engage with and perhaps better position themselves in response to the authoritative discourses. Theses discourses, as mentioned earlier, carry with them values specific to the community from which they originated. Might there be a way of interacting with subjects from positions outside the requirements of the discipline? Reflexive deliberation encourages students to confront these discourses from "alternative standpoints, to discuss assets and liabilities, and to create alternative interpretations."30 It provides alternative angles from which students and teachers can explore a subject or topic. Additionally, students may be "encourage[d] to help in planning curriculum, to bring their own experiences to bear on the classroom material, and to collect materials that might help them to reach their own conclusions."31 In turn this promotes "pedagogies of liberation" and "educational practices that encourage students to engage in active critique, empowering them to join in determining their future as opposed to swallowing the truth as given."32

Collaborative classrooms move instruction away from the monologue and towards dialogic interactions. Traditionally we might accept the various disciplines and bodies of knowledge as areas to understand, master or perfect. In this sense, knowledge is still participatory, but it travels is a single direction -a monologue. In a collaborative classroom we might instead "think of the disciplines as offering resources that may or may not be valuable depending on a particular condition of life [...] Others are invited into deliberation about the subject matter of education, its value, and relevance."33

Rather than participating in a hierarchical model of education, we might find alternatives to traditions of professional and authority based knowledge. These efforts are aimed at separating the curriculum from the obligations of individual and distinct disciplines. Here we see a practice of using "consensus groups" which are groups "challenged with answering in their own terms questions posed by various text

[...] However, the group must reach a consensus which they are willing to share with other groups. This means that the group must learn how to deal with disagreements-sometimes extreme-in generating an opinion. They must learn to live in a world of multiple realities."34

Polyvocal pedagoy promotes multiple voices in education. It is an attempt to empower those who have traditionally been excluded from knowledge production: teachers, administrators, students and the community.35 Similar to Gergen's third premise of social construction, this effort is aimed in response to the recognition that knowledge is always knowledge from a particular vantage. It is an exercise in the awareness that (as stated earlier) there is no means of favoring one truth or one reality over another that exists independent of a certain cultural perspective.

A belief in knowledge as participatory provides that individuals do not hold or own knowledge and its contents. Instead, individuals participate in knowledge. As outlined earlier, if there is no version of truth that exists outside of community, then it would follow that knowledge is participatory both in how it is generated and maintained. In an institution sympathetic to constructionist theories, the participation in knowledge flows equally between teacher, student, and subject- it is fluid and unidirectional.

Construction at Avalon

Where and with what intention do we see constructionist pedagogical alternatives within the environment and curriculum of Avalon?

In a school you might ask, what's the purpose of the whole thing? Is it to transmit, to educate, or as Piaget would have it, should our efforts be directed toward the "full development of the human personality?"36 Simpler yet, might the purpose be to create learning communities based on mutual respect and reciprocal relationships? If we start by thinking of it in terms of what is valued and in the terms of an organizing metaphor, what is the nature of our relationships? How do they define the community? How do they embody the purpose?37

At Avalon the mission is concrete but the process is fluid and student-specific. Whatever it is that is being done at Avalon, it appears very much in line with the tendencies of social construction. Those who set the stage for the community made room for constructionist approaches to teaching, learning, and recognizing relationships within the school.

In the traditional model you have the teacher, adults, and society who hold the knowledge and they transmit the knowledge in one direction to the individual. From there the individual regurgitates it back to show the teacher that they have learned it. This is different from a constructionist model where you have a triangle with the students at one point, the adults (teachers) at a second point, and the learning experiences at the third point. In this model the arrows flow in both directions between each point -not unidirectional.[38]

Project Based Learning

Life is a series of projects-concrete and abstract; novel and cyclical; separate and intersecting. In some sense its how we've been wired to learn from the start. When they are five years old children are doing all kinds of projects. Look at the nature of their play, it's interdisciplinary, topic oriented, and fashioned from multiple mediums. Whether it's a child playing with blocks or a group of kids in the backyard picking up sticks and stones, building narratives and creating fantasies, its project oriented on one level.[39]

The ways in which we learn to participate in and negotiate the world around us is rooted in the process of projects. We learn by doing. Through projects we explore, and in our new ventures we have no option but to learn, and in learning we invent. Imagine the first time preparing a resume, making love, filing taxes, or founding a school.

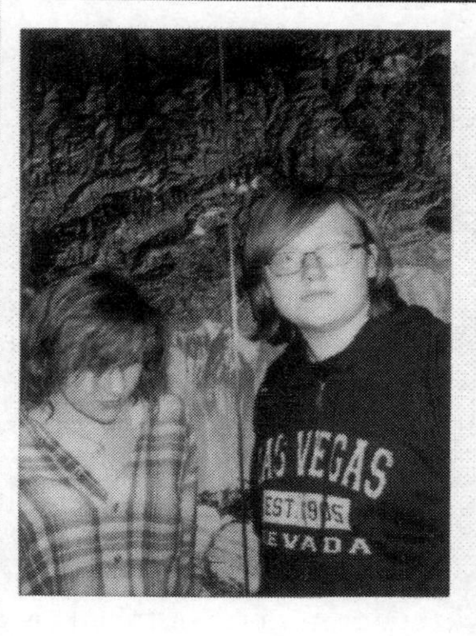

At Avalon, students spend most of their time working on projects. What begins in the earlier grades as a series of smaller projects soon grows to the year-long requirement for all seniors: a 300-hour project accompanied by a formal, public presentation.[40] For students, the process begins by meeting with two advisors to brainstorm project ideas, details, and how it will meet various graduation standards. From there, the student develops the rubric that outlines how their project will be evaluated. Within each project proposal is an outline and plan that "specifies at least three basic questions that the student wants to answer by doing the project; at least two ways the project is important to the community or world; a schedule of tasks and activities that the student will complete; and three or more resources the student will use, at least one of which must be a person."41 The deliverables for each project, depending on the scope and duration can range from a policy paper, to a panel discussion, to a documentary film-the format is open for negotiation.

Examples of project-based learning include a senior who's project compared the narratives in the book Lies My Teacher Told Me: Everything Your American History Book Got Wrong with the content of other history books commonly used in high school classrooms. The deliverable for the project was a keynote presentation that she presented to students, parents, and the community during presentation night as well as at a Hamline University symposium on charter schools. This particular project met "state curriculum standards both in American history and American literature."42

In another example, a student in her junior year completed a project that investigated factory farming in the food industry. The findings were presented in a research paper that examined techniques of factory farming, laws and regulation in the meat industry, and the properties of hormones and antibodies common to factory farming. This paper was used in her college application materials and met "standards in biology, environmental science, history, and civics."43

Creating the Avalon Constitution

True to constructionist ideals in education, a seminar was created in the school's founding year titled "Creating the Avalon Constitution." This project-centered seminar included twenty students and one advisor. Scanning what came of the final document you'll find a preamble, articles on the three branches, procedures for making amendments, and a bill of rights and responsibilities -yes, the United States constitution was used as a guide.

Perhaps more interesting than the contents of the project, is the process by which it was constituted. What was initially planned to take a single term soon grew to twice that. The arguments over distributions of power, the school's decision making process, and appropriate rights and responsibilities took months. Reflecting on the process, seminar leader Carrie Bakken remembers "at one point, we locked ourselves in a room for two days every week and deliberated."44 Just how they reconciled the various interests, positions and ideologies during this "convention" was left to the conversations, negotiations, and creative problem solving of the group.

Reflecting personally, the only vivid memory I have of the US Constitution in school was from a course in 10th grade. The assignment was to memorize the preamble and several sections of Article I to be recited in front of the class the following morning. I fumbled through a few lines before returning to my seat to watch the rest of the class have go at it, one by one. It was an exercise in rote memorization and potential embarrassment, and while certainly educational in that capacity, it arguably left no student in the class with a better understanding of the history or the process through which the document was created. That said, in Avalon's approach, the prospect of being responsible for reconciling the positions, visions, and interests of various individuals doesn't sound entirely pleasant either, but it does sound like a practical lesson is group dynamics, democracy, and conflict resolution.

I guess this brings us back to the question of purpose. If the purpose is to expose students to the preparatory motions, emotional strain, and exercises in speaking from memory in front of an audience, using the Constitution as a vehicle for that seems fair. If the purpose is to learn something about the history and significance of the document, memorization seems about as appropriate as counting the stars in hopes of better understanding principles in astronomy.

Returning again to what it means for an institution to have a constructionist worldview, we find a tendency of process and projects to embody what they are expressing. There is an emphasis on learning through, instead of learning about or learning for. An example of the first is letting students write their own constitution, establish a congress, and participate in a living democracy. An example of the second and third might be the instruction of students about the history and contents of the US Constitution for an upcoming history examination. At any rate, the message is clear in Avalon's estimation that "too often school is something done to students, not with them."45

Seminars

Seminars look much like a traditional class in so much as their delivery is for a group of students around a certain theme or topic. Thinking of seminars at Avalon as supplemental or ad hoc learning communities might frame it better. These communities can be born from necessity or to address a specific need (such as a multi-term seminar to write the school's constitution). They can also be supplemental and occur with more regularity, such as a graded math seminar, or instruction on using Microsoft Excel. Others are structured so as to incorporate a variety of skills and disciplines.

One such example is Nora Whalen's 2001 seminar titled "This is the Place!" which sought to gain an understanding of the neighborhood around the school through oral histories and research. The six week seminar started on opening day, and it was designed for students as an exploration and historical inquiry into the Midway Neighborhood of St. Paul that surrounded the school. The syllabus provides a goal for students to realize a better understanding of place through "observation, dialogue, and discussion of readings on community and the city, research of individual institutions, and most importantly, interviews with neighbors."46 The seminar outcomes and the process by which the students worked together used a familiar constructionist approach. Even explicit in the course materials was the proposition that "through observation we will define values and traditions in the institutions around us."47

Innovative Curriculums

Similar to the practice of collaborate classrooms, the process of engaging students in designing a curriculum could follow a variety of routes. An example of a traditional curriculum building might be to start with a subject or discipline and then finding projects that fit the learning objectives within that area. Here, the process of brainstorming, project planning, and question generation follow a path of integrating topics in terms of subject area. For example, if we begin with the umbrella of environmental science we might arrive at project ideas such as exploring the effect of plants on erosion or the chemical analysis of rainwater. Projects in civics might include an investigation of Supreme Court cases and the Constitution, or following a bill through congress.48

With a constructionist approach to building an innovative curriculum, the starting point of subjects and disciplines is abandoned. The constructionist approach employs the power of free association. What does this process look like? Let's imagine, for example, the topic of "transportation." From here, free association might lead to questions concerning the wheel, to the wheels found on bicycles, to spokes, to diameter, to the circumference of a circle. Hey, we all know the area of a circle is πr2, who came up with that idea? What is the history? With this approach, little to no attention is reserved for recognizing or playing within the prescribed boundaries of subject area. Instead, we are left to imagine ways of incorporating the values of multiple traditions and communities of thought.49

Perhaps if we were to take this one step further, we might move to a purely inquiry-based approach. In this model we begin with a teacher-provided topic, let's again use "transportation", and from there the students might generate questions relating to the topic. Why did the horse and carriage come before the steam engine? Who invented the automobile?50 Again there is a disregard for disciplinary boundaries. The construction of a learning environment and curriculum when accessed through an inquiry-based approach is fluid, flexible, and bottom-up in its orientation.

With constructionist pedagogies, the relational ideal would be one in which the student "emerges with expanded potentials for effective relating. The student's role shifts from that of an object to be improved to a subject within relationships."51 At Avalon this is recognized and it is central to the educational environment.

Beyond Avalon

From the start Avalon was built with an attention to perspectives in social construction. It had the luxury, perhaps like most schools at some point in their history, to constitute a community from scratch. Theirs was a beginning that in many respects was goal oriented and in others was remarkably improvisational. Like all of our first endeavors, it was a project of vulnerability, patience, and persistent invention. A fresh start makes creating something like an Avalon easier in the sense that new efforts are not going against the momentum of the present. Easier too is the ability to build without having to first tear down; the opportunity to expand without having to first retract.

Certainly there are schools and institutions that have the spirit and wherewithal to deeply reshape their organization, curriculum, and refocus a commitment to constructionist and relational practices. However, I'd imagine the majority of traditional institutions are not in this position. For those schools that want to incorporate elements of social construction and relational practice in their community and curriculum, what methods could be employed at a lower institutional cost, and packaged in a way that compliments the current educational environment? What approaches present at Avalon could exist outside of a coherently constructionist setting? Three ideas come to mind. Without too much effort institutions could adopt a commitment to lowering disciplinary boundaries, a dedication to learning through doing, and an increased accountability towards relationships.

It feels a bit clinical and strangely prescriptive in how we compartmentalize chemistry, literature, math, and the other subjects within the walls of distinct and separate classrooms. In some sense the products of these disciplines are removed from our lives and abstracted-geometry becomes hypothetical, biology becomes lifeless. Knowledge is packaged and administered impractically. It is taught in such a way that "one cannot easily employ the argots of physics, economics, experimental psychology, or algebra in cultural life more generally because their meanings are so fully tied to a domain of academic usage."52 Perhaps the disciplined-centered orientations towards knowledge could be made less severe. One way to lower these boundaries is to practice using innovative curriculums of construction and inquiry. Instead of letting the subject determine the lesson, perhaps the students could engage in free association, inquiry, and brainstorming to find projects that later find footing in educational requirements.

We learn through doing. When students are engaged in something that embodies what is being expressed, they have the opportunity to participate in deeper learning. It seems the older that kids become in American education, the more they work independently within a group setting. Familiar is the syllabus, the shuffling from content-specific room to content-specific, the groups of students working their way through a book of material, and the individualization. There are ways to work collectively and still hold each student accountable. Remember, the medium is the message. The context, the format, and the learning environment convey lessons louder than the content itself. If the medium is the message, we should find ways to learn through doing. Instead of service learning, schools could focus on academic service learning. An academic thread requires more planning and more attention, but it is a way to embody what is being expressed. For example, in addition to taking an afternoon to clean up trash from a nearby stream, why not measure pH levels of the water, take soil samples, catalogue the types of trash they find, construct a map of the area. Are there ways to incorporate planning, implementation, and evaluation along with service? Instead of learning for and learning about, are there ways to learn through? 53

Perhaps most important is an increased accountability and attention to relationships. As we've explored, relationships are where we generate and sustain meaning. There is no moment prior to a relationship in which our actions hold any intelligible importance. Another way of putting it is to say that the "actor never comes into meaning save through the supplementary actions of another."54 With this is mind, schools might turn to embracing the relationship between teacher, student, and subject. The focus is not teacher-centered nor is it student-centered, instead it is participatory centered. Without removing the teacher's authority and responsibility as in loco parentis,55 we might still find ways to span the division between teacher and student. Instead of viewing knowledge as concrete and as something to acquire, instruction could move towards a contributory model-towards a belief of knowledge as participatory.56

The constructionist position provides lessons not only for settings in private and charter school education. Emphasizing the value of relational responsibility and recognizing the ways in which our realities are constructed through community offers new approaches to working together in a variety of environments. When we find our islands of individuality to be built from the elements of relationships and deeply rooted in the social world, perhaps we treat others differently, perhaps we treat ourselves differently.

1 Bakken C., Whalen N., & Sage-Martinson, G. (2011). The Origins of Avalon. (p. 3)
2 Avalon Post Card (2001).
3 Avalon School. (2016). XQ Super School Project Application. (p. 1).
4 Kyte, C. (2012). Realizing Deeper Learning: The Economics and Achievements of an Innovative Chartered School Model. The William and Flora Hewlett Foundation. (p. 6).
5 Id. at 115
6 Avalon School. (2016) XQ Super School Project Application.
7 Cassellius, B. (2015). Teacher Supply and Demand. Fiscal Year 2015 Report to the Legislature. (p. 48).
8 Kyte, C. (2012). Realizing Deeper Learning: The Economics and Achievements of an Innovative Chartered School Model. The William and Flora Hewlett Foundation. (p. 5).
9 (2015). Avalon School Annual Report 2014-2015. (p. 11)
10 More on this in Chapter 3: Creating the Avalon Constitu-

tion.

11 (2014-15). The Constitution of the School of Avalon. (p.3).

12 (2010). Design Essentials Checklist. http://www.edvisions.com/custom/SplashPage.asp

13 Id.

14 Id.

15 Constructionist philosophies will be covered in Chapter 2: Social Construction (Descriptive).

16 (2010). Design Essentials Checklist. http://www.edvisions.com/custom/SplashPage.asp

17 Id.

18 Bakken C., Whalen N., & Sage-Martinson, G. (2011). The Origins of Avalon. (p. 8).

19 Castelló, M., & Botella,L. (2006). Constructivism and educational psychology. In J. L. Kincheloe & R. A. Horn (Eds.),The Praeger handbook of education and psychology (Vol. 2, pp. 263-270).

20 Gergen, K. (1999). An Invitation to Social Construction. (p. 138).

21 Gergen, K.. (1999). Relational Responsibility: Resources for Sustainable Dialogue. (p. 22).

22 Searle, J. (1995). The Building Blocks of Social Reality. In The Construction of Social Reality. (p. 1).

23 Id. at 4

24 Gergen, K. (1999). Toward Relational Selves. In An Invitation to Social Construction. (p. 124).

25 Gergen, K.. (1999). Relational Responsibility: Resources for Sustainable Dialogue. (p. 19).

26 Id. at 13

27 Id. at 21

28 Gergen, K. (1999). An Invitation to Social Construction. (p. 180 - 184).

29 Id.

30 Id. at 181

31 Id.

32 Id.

33 Gergen, K. (1999). An Invitation to Social Construction. (p. 182).

34 Id. at 183

35 Id. at 181

36 Piaget, J. (1948). To Understand is to Invent. The Future of Education. (p. 87).

37 Enloe, Walter. Personal interview. 12 April 2016.
38 Id.
39 Id.
40 Bakken, C. (2016). XQ Super School Project. (p. 4).
41 Enloe W., Newell R. (Date Unknown). Giving Students Ownership of Learning. (p. 3).
42 Id. at 1
43 Id.
44 Bakken, C. (DATE). Constituting a Democratic Learning Community: The Avalon Experience. (p. 3).
45 Avalon School. (2016). XQ Super School Project Application. (p. 1).
46 Whalen, N. (2001). Course Syllabus for This is the Place! (p.1).
47 Id.
48 Enloe, Walter. Personal interview. 5 April 2016.
49 Id.
50 Id.
51 Gergen, K. (2001). Social Construction in Context. (p. 134).
52 Gergen, K. (2001). Social Construction in Context. (p. 126).
53 Enloe, Walter. Personal interview. 13 May 2016.
54 Gergen, K. (2001). Social Construction in Context. (p. 119).
55 "In loco parentis" translates to "in place of the parent" and means that the teacher takes over the authority and responsibilities of the parent in their absence.
56 Enloe, Walter. Personal interview. 13 May 2016.

*This writing is an abridged version of Dialogues: Social Construction and Avalon School submitted to Hamline University, Spring 2016.

Made in the USA
San Bernardino, CA
31 October 2016